Police
in the Metropolis

Metropolitan America: Its Government and Politics Series

Under the Editorship of

Alan K. Campbell

Dean of the Maxwell Graduate School of Citizenship and Public Affairs

Police
in the Metropolis

David C. Perry
The University of Texas at Austin

CHARLES E. MERRILL PUBLISHING COMPANY
A Bell & Howell Company
Columbus, Ohio

Material from *City Police* by Jonathan Rubinstein reprinted with permission of Farrar, Straus and Giroux, Inc. © 1973 by Jonathan Rubinstein.

Published by
Charles E. Merrill Publishing Company
A Bell & Howell Company
Columbus, Ohio 43216

ISBN: 0-675-08766-X

Library of Congress Catalog Card Number: 74-83896

1 2 3 4 5 6 7 8 9—83 82 81 80 79 78 77 76 75

Printed in the United States of America

To Terry

. . . whose love makes a discussion
of police seem irrelevant.

Contents

List of Tables

Preface

Until the late 1950s and especially into the 1960s, it was relatively rare for issues of urban life to engage the interests of social scientists at anything but the most peripheral edges of professional interest. When they did turn their attention to the patterns and issues of urbanism, such discussion rarely extended beyond a most perfunctory description of urban life and the accompanying patterns of politics.

There were many reasons for such a lack of interest, not the least of which was the fact that until around 1920 the majority of American citizens still did not live in urban areas. Second, this new urban awakening was quickly overshadowed by the all-consuming economic problems accompanying the nation's attempt to shake off the Depression, followed by the international crises attendant to fighting a global war.

Hence, it was not until the 1950s that both politicians and scholars found time to seriously turn their attention to the growing domestic issues raised by an industrialized and "newly urbanized" nation. No sooner did we realize that we were a "nation of cities" than it became apparent that we were something else as well. By 1960, the U.S. Census demonstrated that while 69.9 percent of the country resided in urban areas, fully 66.6 percent of the nation resided in "metropolitan areas." In fact by 1964, of this large majority of the population living in what two authors have come to call "Metropolitan America," [1] there were fewer people living in the cities of metropolitan areas than in their "suburbs."

The politics of these years closely shadowed the rapid shifts in population. Trying to catch up, the federal government moved swiftly, if not always decisively, in such areas as education, voters' rights, aid to cities, regional planning, welfare, and law enforcement service in a frantic attempt to meet the changed pattern of the domestic environment. Similarly, social science mirrored governmental interest in the emerging domestic patterns. A list of the various books, papers, reports, and articles which have emerged in the past twenty-five years could easily fill the pages of this book.

Such an explosion in academic interest has not yielded a single theory of metropolitanism within any particular discipline of the social sciences

---

[1] Alan K. Campbell and Seymour Sacks, *Metropolitan America: Fiscal Patterns and Governmental Systems* (New York: The Free Press, 1967).

or across the disciplines, even though there is no dearth of studies which rely heavily, if not solely, upon one or another particular disciplinary theory to "explain" a certain metropolitan characteristic. However, "subject-oriented" treatments of the metropolitan phenomenon and the spectacular problems which accompanied such growth have spurred social scientists and social critics alike to describe both particular social ills and more generalized descriptions of the metropolis without regard for disciplinary or theoretical loyalty. Their purpose, to generalize for the sake of this introductory discussion, has been not so much to articulate a "Political Science of Urban Politics" or an "Economics of Urban Ghettos," but to explore the nature of urban ghettos or metro politics for its own sake. Such a purpose has been, of necessity, multidisciplinary, forsaking the pure utility of disciplinary development as a goal, in exchange for the use of the accouterments of a discipline as a tool to further substantive understanding of the empirical phenomena of the metropolis.

Among those who could be counted in this category are the metropolitan policy analysts, who have concerned themselves by and large with a particular subarea of citizen demand or metropolitan governance. They usually employed data and characteristics of the metropolitan environment as a base for or analysis of a particular policy issue. In short the metropolitan phenomena are used to explain a particular service problem. Inasmuch as this book is concerned with police and metropolitanism, it fits this pattern.

In other respects, this volume will differ from other policy treatments of metropolitan law enforcement. It will attempt to isolate and illuminate some of the substantive issues associated with the problems of law and order. At the same time, police service will be used as a vehicle to better explicate past growth and present conditions which characterize metropolitanism. Hence the book has two overarching goals: it will endeavor to present a comprehensive and hopefully accurate description of the policies of law enforcement in the metropolis and to use the discussion as an avenue for explaining metropolitan America in general. Perhaps the patterns of growth of police will be seen as a "Rorschach" of the growth of metropolitanism.

This book is comprised of three parts. Part one, *Introduction and Beginnings,* introduces the reader to the particular perspective of the book and to the historical evolution of the police function in the United States. The first chapter of part one is designed to acquaint the reader with the overall framework within which the subject matter of the book is fleshed out. In this chapter the general hypothesis of the police service as a "Rorschach" or dynamic analogue of metropolitanism is presented along with introductory descriptions of the "police function" and "metropolitanism." The second chapter in this part details the historical development of the police function in selected communities. The thesis of this chapter is that the history of police departments in the United States closely paralleled and even influenced the development of communities as they evolved from town to city and, eventually, to metropolis. While the evidence put forth in this chapter will be useful in informing the discussion which follows, it should be emphasized that the argument here is offered more as a hypothesis than as a definitive statement. This caveat is entered at this juncture because the author is not a historian, the nature of this volume necessitates that a historical perspective be brief, and literature available on the history of urban police in America is limited.

Part two of the book is entitled *Definitions and Caricatures*. Perhaps one of the easiest ways to distinguish between the academic and popular explanations of a public service function, such as police service, is to review the gaps existing between the ways in which the social scientists and the citizens on the street define and characterize the policy issues and the roles of state officials addressing such issues. Such basic junctures of disagreement incur a rash of criticisms about "ivory tower intellectuals" with no real understanding of "where it's really at." Yet, such pointed absence of common world view leads the academic to argue that the present application of public policy lacks direction and is counterproductive. In the case of the police function, there are different sets of definitions and characteristics attached to the function by those in academia and those in the streets.

Such discrepancy is understandable as it is doubtful that a single comprehensive definition of the police function is possible or desirable. The two chapters in this part concern definitions of academics and caricatures of metropolitan residents in an effort to clarify (or outline) the most important and informative definitions of the complex police function to introduce the issues of policing in the metropolis. The first chapter, *Definitions: Academic Perspectives on the Police Function*, discusses the consternation academics exhibit over the "special nature" of the police function. Some scholars view police officers as agents of social control. Others are concerned with differentiating the service role of the police into the categories of law enforcement and order maintenance. Still others find both of these approaches to the police officer to be limited and view the police officer in a reified light as an "arm of public authority." Each of these definitions has limitations, and none of them are mutually exclusive. However, each affords the student of police policy a particular perspective of the police function which is descriptively informative and analytically utilitarian.

The chapter entitled *Caricatures: Citizen Perceptions of the Police Function* concentrates on various popularized perceptions of the police such as the "Dick Tracy" or "crimefighter" image, the army of "pigs" or collective violence image, and the image of police as "crooks." Each of these images is stereotypical and unrealistic, yet justified by the behaviors of some members of police departments.

These characterizations of police reflect some of the major issues facing law enforcement today. Concomitant to the discussion of the "crimestopper" image is the problem of crime incidence in American metropolises. Elections of recent years, from the national to the local level, have been fought around the issue of violent crime, which seems to go unchecked in large measure. Discussing the police officer as part of an army to quell or suppress collective violence introduces the issues of collective civil disobedience and the resulting view that the police officers, sworn to "keep the peace," are often viewed as "oppressive" representatives of a politically "evil" government. The problems of racial antagonism and resentment of white police serving as an "occupying army" in nonwhite neighborhoods and communities cannot be overlooked. The nature of corruption in the police departments in metropolitan areas is part and parcel of the history of the police function and the ambivalent position afforded such a public official since the American Revolution.

In the part of the book entitled *Police and the Metropolis*, a model of social, economic, and governmental spread and diversity is used as a base for explaining the governance, social acceptance, and behavior of the police in metropolitan areas. In chapter 5, *Police and Governments in the Metropolis*, the nature of governmental fragmentation and overlapping jurisdictions is discussed. The confusion which characterizes the governance of metropolitan areas in general is found to an even greater degree among the various units of law enforcement operating in specific metropolitan areas. To study the financing of police service in metropolitan areas is to take a representative tour through the morass of financial inequities and diversities over all metropolitan public services. The study of the financing and governance of police departments at the local level serves as a heuristic case study for the more generalized problems of metropolitan governance and resource allocation as well as a study of the particular administrative and fiscal dilemmas which convolute law enforcement politics.

The final chapter, *The People' and the Police*, concerns detailing the behavioral reactions and problems of police on the street with the patterns of social spread and diversity. At the street level the police officer acts as both a "rorschach" and a lightning rod of the visible and often volatile components of urban politics.

Acknowledgments

In the process of writing this book I have become deeply indebted to many people, only a few of whom I can thank in this short space. Let me emphasize that in crediting these people for their help and/or direct support I, in no way, shift to them any blame for errors which may appear here. I take all responsibility for any shortcomings to be found in these pages.

This book has taken me from the antiseptic halls of academe to the streets of several cities and back again. While in the street, I learned much from Johnny Monroe, Thomas Hastings, and David Hahn and a host of others too mumerous to mention here. In the writing of this book certain scholars, through their works, had an important influence on my thinking and on the actual form this book has taken. An intellectual debt is due James Q. Wilson, Herbert Jacob, Harlan Hahn, and Jonathan Rubinstein. A particular debt is owed to Alan K. Campbell who remains an important overall intellectual influence. In this project he painstakingly reviewed every page of the manuscript. In a similar vein, Joe Feagin performed yeoman service by reading and critiquing the entire book.

The contribution of Judy Hightower to the book is substantial. Ms. Hightower spent innumerable hours editing early drafts and arguing against or supporting various facets of the book. Virginia Schneider typed and retyped more drafts than I care to remember.

At Charles Merrill, there were various people who took special interest in the book. First Roger Ratliff and then Fred Kinne ushered the project along and, finally, Linda Gambaiani edited the completed product. When all is said, from the beginning to the end, there was always Terese, my wife. Without her friendship and constant presence *Police in the Metropolis* would not be.

David C. Perry

PART I

Introduction and Beginnings

Introduction: Police Service as a Rorschach of Metropolitanism

1

Police as a "Rorschach"

The past twenty-five years have been a period of demographic change, representing, perhaps, the most tumultuous epoch of internal political, economic, and social change in America since the Civil War. The growing pains of a newly urbanized nation, turned metropolitan, have been felt in a myriad of ways. Intensified industrialization with the attendant complexities of technology and specialization forced rural inhabitants into the cities and affected significant changes in employment opportunity.

Simultaneously, the intensification of ethnic and racial diversity in the confined boundaries of our metropolises precipitated discernible fissures in the social texture of the nation. Rapid shifts in the location of industrial plants and labor markets have had contingent effects on the ability of municipalities and other local jurisdictional agencies to raise the fiscal resources to meet new service demands, while local governments have proliferated, resulting in fragmented and often insubstantial service districts.

The results of such changes in social, economic, and political patterns have been disparity in educational services, inadequate planning for future growth, crises of racial discrimination in housing and employment, and crime. Such conditions fostered a politics of the street which encompassed a full phalanx of civil disturbances (sit-ins, marches, riots, strikes, school boycotts, guerrilla violence), which are street-level manifestations of the larger patterns of metropolitan change and the basic problems associated with such change.

While it is not clear that these patterns of political behavior are necessarily evidence of the general disorder of metropolitanism in this nation, they are most certainly graphic illustrations of a segment of a contemporary issue which has come to be called the problem of law and order. Some view such actions as criminal or, at best, civil violations of domestic order. This group categorizes acts of racial anger and civil disobedience with other incidents of increased crime rates and cite this as evidence of a need for more law and order to guarantee safety in the streets. Others see acts of violence and disobedience perpetrated by certain groups as political and part of a rising revolutionary consciousness.[1]

At the nucleus of the rhetorical and intellectual debate as to the precise analysis of the civil distress inherent to such patterns of metropolitanism are the police. Arthur Niederhoffer states that

> the policeman is a "Rorschach" in uniform as he patrols his beat. His occupational accouterments—shield, nightstick, gun and summons book—clothe him in a mantle of symbolism that stimulates fantasy and projection. . . . To people in trouble the police officer is a savior. In another metamorphosis the patrolman becomes a fierce ogre that mothers conjure up to frighten their disobedient youngsters.[2]

The police officer is more than a caricature of the "cops and robbers" fantasies of youth, he is the most visible of all public servants. Public servants such as welfare workers, social workers, school teachers, and the like are visible to select members of the populace when encountered to fulfill select needs. The police officer (whether we are desirous of his many services or not) is continually on display—on the street corner directing traffic, nudging our consciences as we drive, and making daily headlines in our newspapers. No other public servant walks the streets with uniform and gun performing tasks which appear uninteresting and mechanical, yet encompass the most basic litany of governmental functions and values. As one scholar puts it, the police service is the fundamental means by which

---

[1] Eugene D. Genovese, "The Legacy of Slavery and the Roots of Black Nationalism," in Edward Greer, *Black Liberation Politics: A Reader* (Boston: Allyn and Bacon, 1971), p. 58.

[2] Arthur Niederhoffer, *Behind the Shield: The Police in Urban Society* (Garden City, N.Y.: Doubleday, 1967), p. 1.

many of a nation's highest values are transmitted to the public. Concepts such as law, order, authority and justice might convey the appearance of remote abstractions, but in modern society the principal public official authorized to apply those standards to social conduct is the policeman.[3]

Each person is jealously concerned with the personal acceptance and protection of his own style of social conduct. The police officer is both the protector of and violator of individual values and collective social conduct.

His ambivalent relationship with the socially disparate citizenry of the metropolis is, in part, a result of the complex variety of service roles the officer is expected to carry out. There is really no such thing as a single service role. The patrolman is, among other things, traffic cop, marriage counselor, warrior, housing inspector, and dog catcher. Thus, the service role of the police officer is often a mirror or "rorschach" of personal and collective crises experienced by those living in the metropolis.

The patrolman is the uniformed front-line representative of many governmental services. If there is dissatisfaction with any governmental service such as housing, busing to achieve racial integration, or gas and electric service, citizens are just as likely to call the police to complain as they are to call the particular service agency in question. Thus the frustration of citizens with the broad spectrum of governmental services becomes confused with specific and direct complaints about law enforcement services. In short, the most visible street-level representative of the government, the policeman, often attracts the most attention and acts as not only a "rorschach" of social needs but also as a "lightning rod" of social dissatisfaction.

Apart from such street-level considerations, the police function can also be discussed in governmental and fiscal terms. Individual police departments within a metropolitan area display fragmented and overlapping jurisdictions, divergent levels of resources committed to police, and disparate professional capabilities. These conditions mirror patterns of governmental fragmentation, disparity of fiscal resources, and inconsistent service outputs which characterize metropolitan governments in general and metropolitan service delivery in particular. The jurisdictional and fiscal structures of police service activities may be used as an instrument of description of the metropolitan condition independent of police service.

---

[3] Harlan Hahn, "The Public and the Police: A Theoretical Perspective," in *Police in Urban Society*, ed. Harlan Hahn (Beverly Hills, Calif.: SAGE Publications, 1971), pp. 9-10.

The Police

The remainder of this chapter will detail the use of the terms "police" and "metropolitanism."

Law enforcement service will be discussed from three vantage points: the public image of police; formal and informal behavior of police officials; and the jurisdictional and structural arrangements of police service in the metropolis.

Public Image

It is difficult to isolate the public's definition of the law enforcement function because there is no completely accurate means to measure how the metropolitan public feels about the effectiveness of police service. However, if a citizen perceives police service behavior as different from his expectations, his image of the police function will be critical. The greater the polarity of perception and expectation, the more critical the public image will be.

A person who feels that his expectations of police service are being met will be supportive of the police function as he perceives it. A citizen who feels "unsafe" may desire an intensification of police service to meet his expectations. A citizen's perception of police service is determined by personal experience, observation of police behavior, and interpretation of police behavior by the media. Whether such images of the police are accurate reflections of the legally and structurally prescribed construction of the law enforcement function is basically an irrelevant consideration to citizen attitudes. The inaccuracy of public opinion does not remove the fact that some segment of the public holds such an opinion. It is important to consider the variety of public images of law enforcement, to be cognizant of the roots of these images, and to carefully avoid dismissing them because they appear unrepresentative or inaccurate.

Police Behavior

The law enforcement bureaucracy cannot be treated as a set of institutional arrangements spewing forth a series of policies to be carried out through a hierarchy of regulated rules and roles. Few public bureaucracies display persons executing the public service task as do law enforcement agencies. Organizational reification is difficult when studying the public organization of the police function, consequently the most popular academic operationalization of "police" has been to study the behavior of detectives,[4] sergeants,[5] beat patrolmen,[6] police chiefs,[7] traffic police,[8] and other individual police officials. The approach to such studies has been varied, usually examining such areas as administrative questions of "how to do it better," issues of racism and brutality, the nature of decision making found in one type of department or another, and the formal and informal patterns of behavior of the police officer on the beat. Police officers' relations with one segment of the public have been explored in a rash of studies concerning police and ghettos. These studies are part of a comprehensive literature on police behavior which will be drawn upon here in an effort to move beyond the past emphasis on the organization of local law enforcement agencies and engage in a discussion of police officers at the street level.

Governance of the
Police Function

There are 45,000 separate police departments in the United States. A substantial number of these agencies are found in metropolitan areas. Almost every county, municipality, township, and village has some type of law enforcement agency. Such agencies vary in size, ranging from New York City with 36,500 employees to townships having only one constable. Some law enforcement chiefs are elected in partisan elections, others are hired by professional selection. Police departments such as county sheriff offices often jurisdictionally overlap lesser forces; yet other police departmental jurisdictions are so circumscribed that their power and authority stop where another jurisdiction starts. The result is an uncoordinated and often wasteful use of service energies and an extreme lack of uniformity in the professional style and modern practice of the police function. Thus, the fragmentation of both the jurisdictions and the structures of law enforcement service results in patterns of overlap, noncooperation, and duplication of activities. These are important factors which must not be overlooked when discussing the police function in metropolitan areas.

---

[4] Jerome H. Skolnick, *Justice Without Trial: Law Enforcement in Democratic Society* (New York: John Wiley, 1967).

[5] James Q. Wilson, "Police Morale, Reform, and Citizen Respect: The Chicago Case," in *The Police: Six Sociological Essays*, ed. David J. Bordua (New York: John Wiley, 1967).

[6] David H. Bailey and Harold Mendelsohn, *Minorities and the Police: Confrontation in America* (New York: The Free Press, 1969), and David C. Perry, "Police Service in a Dual Society: A Study of the Urban Context of Police Service and Its Problems" (Syracuse University, 1971), unpublished manuscript.

[7] James Q. Wilson, *Varieties of Police Behavior: The Management of Law and Order in Eight Communities* (Cambridge, Mass.: Harvard University Press, 1968).

[8] John A. Gardiner, *Traffic and the Police Variation in Law-Enforcement Policy* (Cambridge, Mass.: Harvard University Press, 1969).

In this discussion of metropolitanism there will be no unitary approach to the study of police in the metropolitan area. The behavior of police and the institutionalization of police governments are both relevant operational perspectives when discussing the contemporary police function.

Metropolitanism

Before moving to a discussion of the law enforcement function it will be useful to operationalize the term "metropolitanism." This term is used deliberately because it conveys the feeling of a condition or experience of contemporary living more precisely than do the terms county, town, or city. A metropolitan area can be distinguished from a city or town or county by the fact that it is *not* a governmental unit. Rather, it includes the "entire population in and around the city whose activities form an integrated social and economic system." [9] The U.S. Bureau of the Census defines a Standard Metropolitan Statistical Area (SMSA) as "a county or group of contiguous counties which contains at least one city of 50,000 inhabitants or more, or 'twin cities' with a combined population of at least 50,000." [10]

Contiguous counties which meet the social and economic integrative qualities of the metropolitan condition can be added to the county which contains such a central city. Qualities of the metropolitan condition require that at least 75 percent of the labor force of these bordering counties be employed in nonagricultural activities and that certain levels of residential density be maintained. A variety of criteria including place of residence and place of work between the central county and the outlying counties, newspaper circulation throughout the counties, retail sales, traffic counts, transportation patterns, and cooperative local planning ventures are also offered by the Census Bureau in an attempt to delineate the integrative character of a metropolitan area.[11]

Today some 243 areas of the country fit these characteristics. These qualities are not the static, formal characteristics of government—rather they are the characteristics of the city as it has been lived, and as it has grown and spread beyond its original jurisdictional boundaries. As such, metropolitanism is the umbrella term which characterizes the dynamic spread of urban growth in America in the twentieth century.

---

[9] U.S., Bureau of the Census, *County and City Data Book,* 1962 (a statistical abstract supplement) (Washington, D.C.: Government Printing Office, 1962), p. xi. Emphasis added.

[10] Ibid.

[11] Ibid.

The Growth of
Metropolitanism

The description of metropolitanism cannot be confined to the definition provided by the Census Bureau. While such a definition does identify certain key characteristics of metropolitan areas, other characteristics of the metropolis are untouched. In fact, given the pervasiveness of the metropolitan phenomenon in American life, no definition can be complete.

A metropolitan area may be generally defined as the social, economic, and governmental setting of more than two-thirds of the American population. The metropolitan environment is characterized by patterns of "spread" or a sorting-out process which results in new and continuing patterns of diversity and disparity. Hence, for the purposes of this study, the following basic schematic will be used to further refine the growth and identity of metropolitanism (see fig. 1).

	Characteristics		
Patterns	(1) Social	(2) Economic	(3) Governmental
(A)Spread (The Sorting Out Process)	A-1 Social Spread	A-2 Economic Spread	A-3 Governmental Spread
(B) Diversity (Congruence and Disparities)	B-1 Social Diversity	B-2 Economic Diversity	B-3 Governmental Diversity

Figure 1

An Integrative Model of the General Patterns and Characteristics of Metropolitanism

Social Spread
and Diversity

The most striking factor of the twentieth-century population explosion has been the dramatic growth of the nation's population within metropolitan areas. Using the census definition, in 1900, 42 percent of the nation's population resided in urban areas, whereas today 68.6 percent of the total population reside in metropolitan areas. In the past few decades, the population has increased in metropolitan areas at a rate of about 25 percent per decade while the comparable figure for nonmetropolitan areas is about

---

[12] Advisory Commission on Intergovernmental Relations (ACIR), *Fiscal Balance in the American Federal System: Vol. 2, Metropolitan Fiscal Disparities* (Washington, D.C.: Government Printing Office, 1967), p. 27.

4 percent per decade.[12] Consequently, in discussing general population growth in the United States, one is really talking about growth trends within metropolitan areas (see fig. 2).

As the nation achieved urban status in the first two decades of the twentieth century, the central cities grew at a much more rapid rate than their surrounding areas. However, by the 1930s, the rate of central city growth was only about two-thirds that of the outside areas, and by the 1950s it was only about one-third the rate of suburban growth. The most significant result of this reversal in growth patterns was manifested in or about 1962 when the population of the outside central city areas of the SMSA's breasted and surpassed the population of the central cities (see fig. 3). This shift would have been even more dramatic if it had not been for annexation activity on the part of central cities. The Federal Advisory Commission on Intergovernmental Relations attaches the following note to its discussions of population growth within the central cities:

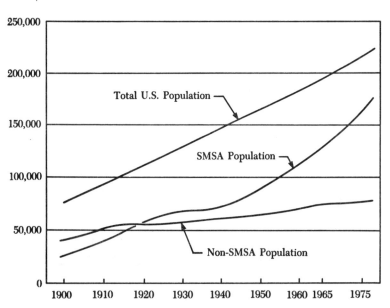

Population
(thousands)

SOURCE: Advisory Commission on Intergovernmental Relations *Fiscal Balance in the American Federal System: Vol. 2, Metropolitan Fiscal Disparities* (Washington, D.C.: Government Printing Office, 1967), p. 29.

Figure 2

The Growth of U.S. Population, 1900–1975

Annexation, which is more common than is generally realized, is responsible for nearly all central city population growth since 1950. . . . Without annexation, the 10.8 percent increase [between 1950–1960] in central city population would drop to 1.5 percent, and the outside central city growth would increase from 48.5 percent to 61.7 percent.[13]

Percent

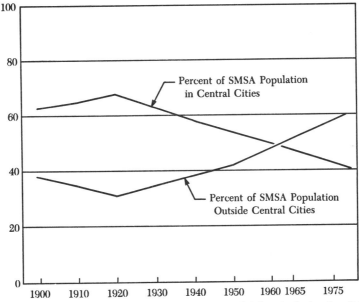

Source: Advisory Commission on Intergovernmental Relations *Fiscal Balance in the American Federal System: Vol. 2, Metropolitan Fiscal Disparities* (Washington, D.C.: Government Printing Office, 1967), p. 29.

Figure 3

Trend in Distribution of SMSA Population Between Central Cities and Outside, 1900–1975

The most dramatic increases in population growth have occurred in the central cities of small metropolitan areas and in the suburbs of large SMSA's. At the same time, patterns of exodus to the suburbs are found in the large central cities of the industrial Northeast and the older cities of metropolitan areas which never grew to major size. Further, the number of black Americans residing in the central city has just about doubled since 1950. Hence a pattern of *dual migration* has occurred in the metropolitan areas of the country, causing a significant diversity of racial balance with the suburbs remaining relatively white and the cities

---

[13] Ibid., p. 31.

becoming increasingly black. While the impact of black migration to the central city was significant for all metropolitan areas, between 1960 and 1970 the impact of dual migration was felt mostly by the largest cities. Even though the rate of black in-migration slowed in the past decade, it is this mobility among black Americans, along with annexation, which accounts for the minimal growth of central cities. For all metropolitan areas, the increase in white central city residents was a bare .7 percent between 1960 and 1970, while the increase of black residents was 31 percent [14] (see table 1-1).

TABLE 1-1

Racial Redistribution in Central Cities of SMSAs,
1950–1970

	White	Black
All SMSA's		
1950-1960°	+4.7%	+50.0%
1960-1970°°	+ .7	+31.0
5 largest central cities		
1950-1960	−6.9	+55.7
1960-1970	−10.0	+38.5

°212 SMSA's as defined by 1960 Census of Population.
°°243 SMSA's as defined by 1970 Census of Population.
SOURCE: U.S., Bureau of the Census, *Statistical Abstract of the United States: 1971*, 92d ed. (Washington, D.C.: Government Printing Office, 1971).

Such shifting racial patterns have been accompanied by significant disparities within the metropolitan environment. The central city has become the place of residence of increasing numbers of low-paid, often unemployed, high-cost citizenry while the outside central city areas have become the residence of highly-paid, low-cost citizenry. As table 1-2 demonstrates, the income disparity between white and black urbanites is substantial.

As of 1969, the income of black metropolitanites was still only 61.8 percent of white income: while this was an increase in the relative position of black residents since 1959 (55 percent of white income), the difference is still significant (table 1-2). In 1969, twice the percentage of black families lived on incomes below $3,000 as did whites (table 1-3), while twice as many white families had incomes over $12,000 than metropolitan black families. The fact that the gap between black income and white income was the greatest in the significantly more affluent suburban areas with a difference of more than $4,200 demonstrates further extension of social diversity cum economic disparities (table 1-2).

---

[14] In fact, in the five largest metropolitan areas the decade of the sixties produced a 10 percent drop in the white population and a 38.5 percent increase in black residency.

TABLE 1-2

Median Family Incomes
(1969)

	White	Black	Black Income as Percent of White Income
SMSA°°	$11,051	$6,832	61.8%
CC	10,426	6,790	65.1
OCC			
Urban	11,829	7,542	63.7
Rural	10,096	5,186	51.3
Outside°			
SMSA			
Farm	6,403	3,063	47.8
Nonfarm	8,548	4,151	48.5

SOURCE: °U.S., Bureau of the Census, *Statistical Abstract of the United States, 1971* (Washington, D.C.: Government Printing Office, 1971), table 506, p. 318.
°°David C. Perry, "Faking it and Making it with the U.S. Bureau of the Census: A Research Note" (Austin: University of Texas, 1974), mimeographed.

Economic Spread and Diversity

With better than two-thirds of the nation's population living in metropolitan areas, it is not surprising that the greatest share of the nation's economic activity is also found in these centers. Such areas are the prime concentrations of industrial activity, job opportunity, and public and private services.

TABLE 1-3

Percentage of Families in Income Levels
(1969)

Item and Income Level	White			Black		
	Total SMSA	CC	OCC	Total SMSA	CC	OCC
Under $3,000	8.1	7.6	4.6	15.9	16.2	14.9
$3,000–$5,999	15.2	15.7	10.7	26.2	26.5	26.0
$6,000–$11,999	41.7	41.1	40.7	40.6	41.3	38.3
$12,000 and over	35.0	35.5	44.1	17.2	16.1	21.2
Total	100.0	99.9	100.1	99.9	100.1	100.1

SOURCE: U.S., Bureau of the Census, *Statistical Abstract of the United States, 1971* (Washington, D.C.: Government Printing Office, 1971), table 506, p. 318.

As of 1960, metropolitan areas contained more than 67.2 percent of all manufacturing firms and 73.8 percent of the total number of industrial employees. Such firms accounted for almost 80 percent of the nation's manufacturing payroll. Further, by 1960, the financial centers of metropolitan areas contained more than 80 percent of all bank deposits. In 1959, 69 percent of all housing starts could be found in metropolitan areas.[15]

The intrametropolitan patterns of dispersion of the various types of economic activity are also important considerations. The central city was once the location of most economic activity, employment opportunity, and consumer service. A variety of recent locational forces including the search for space, market conditions, and transportation arteries have affected the spread of economic activities.

In the case of industrial activity, "Wherever a businessman who has chosen the suburbs over the city is asked to say what prompted the decision, the odds are very high that he will answer the question in terms of a 'search for space'." [16] The center of the most active economic metropolitan area in the nation, New York City, has lost ground in what are considered growing industries and has held its own with those industries categorized as shrinking.[17] Growing industries require not only more factory floor space, they also require different types of buildings. New types of manufacturing technology cannot be mounted in central city garrets—they need buildings designed to accommodate assembly line spread.

Another set of locational forces influencing new spread and diversity of the modern-day metropolis are those factors which could be subsumed under the title of markets (labor market and consumer market). The retail sector of the metropolitan economy follows its consumers. With the migration of relatively affluent white urbanites to the suburbs, the retail and personal service sectors have had to move from the central city as well. The advent of the suburban shopping center is perhaps the most dramatic evidence of this shift in economic activity.

Another visible indicator of such shifts in economic activity are the branch stores. Every service and retail sector has been greatly influenced by the branch phenomenon. Branch stores, branch banks, branch insurance agencies, and branch real estate firms dot the outside central city landscape. The central decision-making activities of such sectors of the economy may still reside in the skyscrapers of the central city, but the front-line, client-

---

[15] Advisory Commission on Intergovernmental Relations (ACIR), *Metropolitan Social and Economic Disparities: Implications for Intergovernmental Relations in Central Cities and Suburbs* (Washington, D.C: Government Printing Office, 1965), pp. 40-41.

[16] Edgar M. Hoover and Raymond Vernon, *Anatomy of a Metropolis* (Garden City, N.Y.: Doubleday, Anchor Edition, 1962), p. 25.

[17] Ibid., p. 26.

oriented activities of these firms have moved to the suburbs following their clientele.

Transportation of the finished product to market is another locational factor. The advent of new highway arteries, the movement of the industries to the central city fringe and beyond, and the movement of retail outlets to the suburbs have affected the wholesaler's place of activity. The wholesale sector is guided by the formula of speed of delivery in terms of lowest cost. Now it is not unusual to see large storage barns and wholesale centers located on the fringe of the city near highway networks and railroad arteries—equidistant from the shrinking economic activities of the central city and the growing industrial and retail activities of the outside central city.

This proliferation of economic activity could not have occurred if the modern metropolis had not also experienced significant improvements in the ability of the labor market to get to work. It is now possible for employees to live increasingly greater distances from their places of employment due to improved highways and, to some extent, rapid transit. In addition, the increase in population living in the suburbs has allowed some small retail firms the luxury of a more proximate labor supply to service branch offices. Conversely, some industrial firms cannot leave the city because their internal economies of scale are so small that they cannot leave the proximate services of the city which they need on a day-to-day basis. Vernon and Hoover discovered that

> time and again we find that small plants are held in the more crowded portions of the region in order to share in some essential produce or service—that they depend, in short, upon the "external economies" of these crowded portions, the economies that a firm can obtain through the use of facilities or services "external" to itself.[18]

In conclusion, the concentrated economic activity of metropolitanism has spread out in diverse patterns attendant to transfiguration of locational needs: factors affecting this change are search for space; improved transportation arteries; relocation of labor and consumer markets; and convenient packaging of external economies.

Inequity in economic opportunity and mobility experienced by businesses in the metropolis parallels disparate occupational opportunity and mobility for metropolitan individuals. The poorest sections of the central city almost always house persons who are twice as likely to be unemployed. Black sectors of the city have unemployment levels which are twice as high

---

[18] Ibid., p. 45.

as white sectors. As table 1-4 demonstrates, the rate of unemployment among black teenagers is even more dramatic with one out of every three found among the ranks of the unemployed. The nature of underemployment is no less striking.

Not only do dwellers in poverty neighborhoods have a higher incidence of unemployment, but they are also more likely to have menial low-paying jobs when working. One-half the employed workers in these areas are in unskilled, semiskilled, and service jobs compared to 35 percent for the nation as a whole; and the lowest end of the occupational scale is disproportionately weighted with Negroes.[19]

Governmental Spread and Diversity

Metropolitan governments, by and large, exhibit patterns of spread and diversity which are often as confusing as the economic and social patterns introduced above.

TABLE 1-4

White and Black Unemployment Rates in Central Cities

	White	Black	Ratio Black to White
1968			
Both sexes, 16 years and over	3.5	7.8	2.2
16 to 19 years	12.3	30.4	2.5
Male, 20 years and over	2.5	6.0	2.4
Married, wife present	1.8	4.5	2.5
Female, 20 years and over	3.5	5.9	1.7
1960			
Both sexes, 16 years and over	4.9	10.7	2.2
16 to 19 years	9.8	22.7	2.3
Male, 20 years and over	4.8	9.9	2.1
Married, wife present	3.4	7.5	2.2
Female, 20 years and over	4.3	10.1	2.3

SOURCE: U.S., Bureau of the Census, *Current Population Reports*, Series P-23, Special Studies, No. 27, "Trends in Social and Economic Conditions in Metropolitan Areas"(Washington, D.C.: Government Printing Office, 1969).

Bollens and Schmandt describe the general condition of governments in the metropolis in the following manner:

No paucity of governments exists in the metropolis. Often invisible to the human eye—but never unknown to the taxpayers' pocketbook—they clutter

---

[19] John C. Bollens and Henry J. Schmandt, *The Metropolis: Its People, Politics and Economic Life*, 2d ed. (New York: Harper and Row, 1970), p. 86.

the landscape in vast number and almost infinite variety. And some types are continuing to become more numerous. The resulting scene is one of many local units, as well as federal and state agencies, functioning in the nation's metropolises and affecting their development and their success or failure in solving particular problems.[20]

These scholars are pointing to three basic characteristics of governments in the metropolitan area: (1) the significant number and variety of governments found in a metropolitan area; (2) the burgeoning and convoluted tax bases offered by such governments; and (3) the overlapping and fragmentation which lead to fragmented and disparitous solutions to the domestic problems these governments are ostensibly chartered to address.

As of 1967, there were 20,703 local governments in metropolitan areas. The traditional concept of a local government in a metropolitan area has it serving a large and populous city or a busy county, yet in reality these governments make up only a small portion of the governments which exist. There are only 221 counties with populations in excess of 100,000, and only 314 municipalities with populations of 50,000 or more. The heavily populated governmental jurisdiction in the SMSA is the exception rather than the rule. Thus the average local government in a metropolitan area contains relatively few people, in fact, as of 1967, such a government serviced only about 5,704 residents.

The most important contributor to such a burgeoning number of governments is the special district government. Special district governments make up 58 percent of all metropolitan governments. Such governments are usually created to provide a single service, such as education (the school district), water, mosquito abatement, or the like (see table 1-5).

TABLE 1-5

Number of Governments in Metropolitan Areas (1962–1967)

	1962	1967
Number of local governments (total)	18,442	20,703
Special district	11,415	12,067
School	6,004	5,018
Other	5,411	7.049
(Without property tax power)	(2,259)	(3,165)
County government	310	404
Municipalities	4,142	4,977
Township government	2,575	3,255

Source: U.S., Bureau of the Census, *Census of Governments, 1967, Vol. I, Governmental Organization* (Washington, D.C.: Government Printing Office, 1968), table 6.

---

[20] Ibid., p. 141.

Fragmentation and overlap conditions of metropolitan governments can best be exemplified by school districts, one of the many special district governments. In table 1-6, it is apparent that the jurisdictional pattern of school service at the metropolitan level exemplifies as many patterns as there are choices of government. The vast majority of school districts service different areas than the main municipalities or county; there are also different governments with their own district taxing powers, governing boards, and the like.

We conclude that the metropolitan areas of this country are governed by a fragmented and disorganized set of governments which provide overlapping and irregular services. The central cities are usually incorporated, general service provision municipalities. They are incorporated in order to provide all services, with the exception (at times) of education, which often is represented by a special district form of government. The outside central city is typically governed by a fractionated panoply of county, special district, small municipal, and township governments—all of which provide the potential surburbanite with a complex array of governmental services depending on the combination of governments which have jurisdiction over his place of residence.

TABLE 1-6

School Districts within SMSAs (1967)

Coterminous without other local	
Government area:	1,334
Countywide	142
Citywide	599
Townshipwide	593
Noncoterminous with other local	
government area:	4,195
Countywide with exceptions	44
Municipal	1,583
Other	2,568

SOURCE: U.S., Bureau of the Census, *Census of Governments, Vol. 1, Governmental Organization* (Washington, D.C.: Government Printing Office, 1968), table 17.

Since social and economic activity as well as a substantial amount of governmental activity can be found within metropolitan boundaries, it is not surprising that "local governments within metropolitan areas in 1962 accounted for 70 percent of the $38.3 billion of general revenue received by all local governments in the United States." [21] At the same time, these governments received only 27 percent more per capita in

[21] Ibid., p. 48.

revenue than did governments outside metropolitan areas. The package of sources of tax revenue, however, differed for the two areas:

> The greatest part of this difference was due to relative reliance on the property tax. Local governments in SMSA's obtained 50 percent of their total general revenue from property taxes, whereas local governments outside SMSA's received 43.6 percent—in money terms, a difference of 36 dollars per capita. On the other hand, local governments in SMSA's received relatively less in state aids than non-SMSA localities: 24.7 percent and 36.7 percent, respectively, or a dollar difference of $9 per person.[22]

The metropolitan citizen differs from the non-metropolitan area resident in that he pays for different packages of governmental services wrapped up in different boundary patterns. He also pays taxes at more highly disparate rates, determined by whether or not he resides in the general service provision sector of the central city, in the unincorporated outside central city area, or in a suburban area of the county which has numerous special district services overlapping it. Out of such mounting confusion have come diverse levels of tax burdens and mismatches of resources and needs in SMSAs (see table 1-7).

TABLE 1-7

Per Capita Fiscal Data for Central Cities—Educational and
Non-Educational Effort—1967
(Weighted Averages for the 37 Largest SMSAs)

	Total		Education		Noneducational	
	CC	OCC	CC	OCC	CC	OCC
Resources						
Per Capita total taxes*	217	172	73	96	144	76
Per capita inter-governmental aid	128	100	48	64	80	36
Expenditures						
Per capita total, Educational and Noneducational expenditures	325	260	111	143	214	117

* Weighted averages for the 34 largest SMSA's, education, and noneducation, since education and noneducation figures for Washington, D.C., Baltimore, and Providence are not available.
SOURCE: Advisory Commission on Intergovernmental Relations, *State and Local Finances: Significant Features, 1967 to 1970* (Washington, D.C.: Government Printing Office, 1969), pp. 68-70.

---

[22] Ibid., pp. 49-50.

The general service provision governments of the central city municipalities are forced to provide a substantially higher level of noneducational
services than the outside central city with its diverse collection of small
municipalities, townships, county governments, and special districts. Table
1-7 documents this conclusion by demonstrating the higher levels of fiscal
outlay (taxes and aid) in the central city as they coalesce to meet the
relatively larger package of core area service demands.

The complex mix of outside central city governments allows the residents
of such areas the comparative luxury of selective spending in such important policy areas as education (table 1-7). Aggregate data permit limited
comparisons of fiscal activity between central cities and suburbs, but
available studies indicate substantial disparities in the respective ability
of the central city and the suburb to meet the public policy demands.
One of these studies points to

> substantial differences in expenditure patterns of central cities and suburbs.
> Highways and education expenditures per capita tend to be higher in the
> suburbs; police and fire protection, welfare, hospitals, urban renewal, public
> housing, and sanitation in the central city. For at least the larger metropolitan
> areas, expenditures, measured in both per capita and percent income terms,
> are higher for the central city than for the rest of the metropolitan area.
> The differences vary from area to area, and among the most significant cases
> of the variations are the differences in state responsibility for direct expendi-
> tures, grants-in-aid and taxes.[23]

Governmental spread and diversity are important factors of metropolitanism. Metropolitanism is characterized by its substantial share of
the nation's population, bank deposits, industrial production, property
values, housing construction, and other measures of wealth; it is also a
process which mirrors and reinforces disparities of unemployment and
underemployment, of median family income, of educational opportunity,
and of racial and ethnic differences as well. A major stumbling block
to unlocking such a reservoir in an effort to attack some of these problems
is the pattern of governments in metropolitan areas. This pattern, complex
and awkward, not only provides the residents of metropolitan areas with
fragmented and overlapping services but also all but guarantees that
services will be financed inequitably and that the patterns of disparate
fiscal efforts and the concomitant mismatch of resources to needs will
continue.

---

[23] ACIR, *Metropolitan Social and Economic Disparities: Implications for Intergovernmental
Relations in Central Cities and Suburbs* (Washington, D.C.: Government Printing Office,
1965), p. 54.

The major task of this book is to provide as broad and representative a picture as possible of the practice of the police function in metropolitan areas. The various patterns of social, economic, and governmental proliferation and diversity outlined in the previous section will form the fundamental framework for this discussion of the police function.

Beginnings: The Historical Development of Police and Metropolitanism   2

The History of the Law Enforcement Function

The history of the United States from colonial days is the story of a nation becoming urban, characterized by recurring debate and confusion over the nature of law and the provision of order. In fact, the proper role of police in urban society remains debatable to this day. In this chapter an attempt will be made to review some of the experiences attendant to the growth of police in the American city. This use of a historical perspective in the study of law enforcement policy not only provides us with an understanding of the growth of the role of police in particular, but also traces the growth of metropolitan America in general.

From the earliest days, a large share of the colonizing experience in the United States was influenced by the tradition of settlement into towns.[1]

---

[1] The process of banding into towns and being governed at the local level by such town arrangements was more the tradition of the New England colonists than the tradition of the southern colonies like Virginia, Maryland, and North Carolina. In these colonies, the primary jurisdiction of local government was the county. More precisely, the unit of government itself was the monthly or county court. This court had as its members commissioners, or justices of the peace, whose job it was to administer the local government and keep the order. The chief administrative officer of the county was the sheriff whose duties then were very similar to his duties today. In Virginia, for example, "he collected the taxes, executed the orders and sentences of the courts and the assembly, made the arrests, summoned jurors and others to court, and served as keeper of the county jails." Oliver Perry Chitwood, *A History of Colonial America* (New York: Harper and Row, 1948), pp. 185 and 184-90.

The original colonists of New England came from England where they were accustomed to the social and economic interactions of towns and cities. Hence settlement in closely knit units of cohabitation was an automatic reflex for those entering a strange and wild environment.

The colonial period was marked by pioneers carving out an existence in a new land and by European nations competing in a struggle for economic might through the imperialist expansion of colonial empires. Imperialistic rulers found advantage in organizing the colonists into towns. These colonists were far from the cream of European society; in many cases they represented the legal and religious castoffs. Their migration served the dual purpose of removing socially undesirable persons from the mother country and providing manpower for the outposts of imperial expansion. The governors of the new colonies were responsible for keeping such people in line. In fact they were often directly instructed to draw the tradesmen and craftsmen among these settlers into the towns.[2]

The use of the town as a unit of social control cannot be attributed solely to such a riffraff theory. A town provided empire builders such as the British crown with the basic unit or focal point of economic control as well. Glabb and Brown point out that:

> In the view of these rulers, the American Colonies were like all other colonies: sources of English wealth and sources also of administrative problems. Colonies were supposed to function as to profit the Empire—or at least to profit the relatively small group which ran the Empire—and for this purpose they had to be controlled; the doings of the energetic colonists had to be overseen. *This task of control could best be carried out if colonial life, and especially colonial economic life, was channeled through a limited number of focal points. . . . So the Crown encouraged, even required, the laying out and chartering of towns in its American possessions. . . .*[3]

These towns, as they spread away from the authorized posts of the Realm, were strategically located in a manner which maximized the colonists' ability to extract natural resources and transmit them swiftly to trade centers of the outside world.

Thus the colonial town, the precursor of our modern-day metropolis, was more than a unit of social heritage. The town was also born out of imperialistic desires to maintain economic and social control. The initial network of towns which later became the eastern megalopolis was a

---

[2] Charles N. Glabb and A. Theodore Brown, *A History of Urban America* (New York: Macmillan, 1967), pp. 1-2.

[3] Ibid. Emphasis added.

macro-level product of the economic and social law and order of seventeenth-century imperialism.

The actual policing of each town, as in England, developed primarily as a local function heavily dependent on the cooperation of the citizenry. It was important to the British crown to protect its investment in the New World and maintain control over its colonial outcasts. Past experiences with policing in English towns conditioned and informed the colonists' acceptance of and problems with the first law enforcement practices in the New World.

If, for the British crown, the growth of the towns meant the ensuring of control over a sprawling empire, for the people who populated the towns the growth of such communities represented more immediate things. Towns represented the only real encounter with governmental authority and control. The design of such public authority and the subsequent experiences with such authority were unclear during the colonial period. Hence, while the colonists came to view the towns as the unit upon which the maintenance of order depended, issues concerning the administration and philosophy of such order eventually became troublesome to the point of manifest revolutionary upheaval in the last quarter of the eighteenth century.

Even with the successful culmination of the Revolution the new Americans continued to grope for effective terminology to describe their rationale for public order. The objective evidence of dispersal of effective authority can be found in the spreading patterns of the towns.[4] The townspeople were concerned with replacing the centrist principles of economic and social control for mercantile gain with the principles of sovereignty of local groups and localities for the consummate gain of the individual or the people. Citizens were also concerned with establishing street-level functionaries who would preserve the right of the individual while protecting the people within the towns. Decisions effecting such governmental authority of respective towns were in part representative microcosms of the national issues of individual rights and governmental design which consumed much of the time and interest of the Founding Fathers.

The fact that a separate and professional corps of policemen came late in the development of the peace-keeping function in the new republic evidences the philosophical hesitancy with which the early Americans addressed the principles of personal liberty. Subsequently, the need for a large full-time police force could no longer be denied in the burgeoning towns and cities of the United States. Often a force tied tightly to urban

---

[4] Michael Zucherman, *Peaceable Kingdoms: the New England Towns in the Eighteenth Century* (New York: Alfred Knopf, 1970), p. 46.

political systems with special mechanisms built in to keep the personnel of the force responsive to predominant interests in the city was developed. The influence of local power interests made the primitive forms of police management essential supports of systems of politics that brought great profit to some powerful men. Hence change was to come at an exceedingly slow rate.

Indigenous to the history of the police function in the United States are recurrent themes of (1) confusion over the nature and design of social control in a society which celebrates the rights of the individual; (2) disagreement over the proper technology of the police function; and (3) demand for reform of a function embroiled in a maze of political intrigue and corruption. It will be the purpose of this chapter to review these trends in order to gain historical perspective on the public policy area we are studying.

The Colonial Period:
1620-1776

From the first days of the Massachusetts Bay Colony, the peace officer was a documented functionary of the colony and the towns in the colony. The General Court of the Colony immediately established the traditional English law officer, the constable, as the townsmán responsible for the "preservation of the peace, [and] the discovery and preventing [of] all attempts against the same." [5] Each town chose its own officer, who remained in the position for one year. The person chosen was bound to serve, just as today people are bound by civic responsibility to serve as jurors. The duties of the constable were arduous and often his responsibilities included situations in which he faced physical attack. The nature of the job, the time it entailed, and the lack of substantial financial remuneration made a constable's job particularly unattractive. If the constable-designate refused to serve or if the constable was found to be negligent in the performance of his duties he could be fined. The law enforcement function was further complicated by the fact that the constable was not provided with paid assistants. In cases where he needed help to accomplish his duties the constable was vested with the power to call upon nearby citizens who were bound, under penalty of fine, to respond to his order.

While the constable was the primary peace officer of the early colonies, other officers were also established. The majority of crimes occurred at night, therefore the colonies established a night watch and a military watch. The military watch was organized to protect the settlement against the

---

[5] Edwin Powers, *Crime and Punishment in Early Massachusetts 1620-1692* (Boston: Beacon Press, 1966), p. 424.

external threat of Indians and the night watch was established to deter internal transgressions against morality.

Members of the night watch were engaged to arrest drunkards and men who did not appear for military training, and to report single women or wives with husbands away who entertained, housed a man, and so on. The problems of drunkenness and tobacco smoking took much of the time of the constable and his night watch. The night watch operated only during the months of May through September, and individuals not wishing to serve on the watch were allowed to hire alternates.

Because of the nature of the job, persons comprising the night watch were usually drawn from the working class or the unemployed. Low status in the community coupled with the legal limitations placed on the watch resulted in rather timid behavior on the part of most watchmen in their efforts to keep the peace.

The nature of crime in the colonies was quite different than crime today. Violence and disorder began to increase in the early eighteenth century with the rise in urban population, but by and large the towns of this era remained small homogeneous communities characterized by strong religious traditions which effectively controlled the behavior of the townspeople. Furthermore, in frontier settlements there was little to steal, and escape was difficult. Therefore the nature of the police function was to effect preservation of morality within the religious fabric of the community in order to protect the homogeneity of values and the solidarity of the community itself.

As settlements grew in the middle and late eighteenth century, the old methods of social control became less effective. Individuals no longer knew everyone else in the community. It became increasingly difficult to control antisocial behavior through the traditions of religious morality and the high visibility of the small-town resident who found it difficult to hide his behavior from his neighbor. Even with the increase of violence and disorder which accompanied the increase in the size of urban communities, the usual response of the city governments was to ignore the disorder or to increase the number, though not the quality, of the constables and the night watch. The old style of voluntary obedience to community norms seemed to become an even greater obsession with the local residents as the enforcement machinery they stubbornly maintained became too weak to preserve order.

Police and Cities:
1776-1880

By the end of the first quarter of the eighteenth century, the urban growth had begun to accelerate substantially. In 1690, 10 percent of the colonial population resided in urban places (areas of more than 2,500 population). However, it was not until 1830 that 10 percent of the population could again be found living in areas of comparable size. In the intervening 140 years, the many thousands of New World settlers had diffused throughout the countryside and into the much smaller town settlements previously discussed. Hence, the population in urban areas, spurred by the end of the Revolutionary War and resumption of rapid immigration, increased steadily after 1790. The number of immigrants was so great that the population of the United States increased by one-third in each decade from 1810 to the start of the next major war in 1860. New and larger urban centers accompanied this boom in population. In 1820 one-third of all city dwellers could be found in New York or Philadelphia, but

> by 1860 . . . there were 101 cities [of 10,000 or more]. . . . including eight which had passed the 100,000 mark and one (New York plus its large suburbs of Brooklyn) which exceeded one million.[6]

Hence, the eighteenth century can be called the century of the town, and the nineteenth century can be characterized as the time when the city grew to be an important factor in American life. The nature of the expanding network of American cities was, in many cases, quite different from that of colonial towns and early colonial urban places. Cities and towns, before the turn of the century, were what Glabb and Brown have called "extractive-commercial" with the urban places lining the Atlantic seaboard, their streets and warehouses leading to the piers. By the 1860s, this network of urban places and the economic *raison d'être* of the cities had changed. With the technological changes attendant to the industrial revolution, cities were no longer bound exclusively to natural seaports and waterways as they were in the colonial period. Alternative forms of transportation such as the horse-drawn bus and the street railways of the 1830s allowed for the rapid expansion in geographic size of the cities. The technological changes in the manufacturing and fabricating of goods allowed many urban places to develop without an overriding dependence on primary product extraction from the surrounding countryside. Hence, settlements such as Pittsburgh, Louisville, and Cincinnati, that were first constituted as agricultural communities, were eventually sustained through substantially different economic activities.

Finally, of no small consequence were the effects of first the canals and then the railroad as these two technological advances expanded and cemented the urban network. It was, by and large, the settlements serviced

---

[6] Glabb and Brown, *History of Urban America*, p. 26.

by such transportation arteries that finally succeeded in becoming the metropolitan areas of today. Other less fortunate towns faded or stagnated. By 1890, the basic railroad arteries of the nation were complete, and the major cities of the nation were established. With few exceptions, the urban places we perceive as the most important centers of activity in the nation were successfully established by 1890.

In large measure, the growth of the urban network in the nineteenth century can be attributed to three basic factors: (1) the change in many urban settlements from a preponderant dependence upon an extractive-commercial economic base to dependence on manufacturing activity brought about by the revolutionary influence of emerging industrialization; (2) rapid developments in transportation technology which introduced the canals, the railroads, and the streetcar; and (3) rapid in-migration of thousands of immigrants not only from England, but also from Italy, Ireland, Germany, and China. These factors precipitated the completion of an urban network stretching from the Atlantic to the Pacific which redefined the urban settlement in ways which the early settlers could never have envisioned. Now cities became large, ethnically heterogeneous, and spread out in patterns including suburban outlands. Patterns characterized by large land area, ethnic and economic diversity, and efficient transportation had a profound effect upon the nature of the law enforcement function in the emerging urban nation.

The primitive colonial arrangements for keeping the peace became extremely antiquated as urban growth accelerated in the early nineteenth century. The efficiency of the colonial constabulary with its dependence on informal control broke down with the increasing size and diversity of the emerging city. Colonial settlements were characterized by ethnic and religious homogenity which reinforced the face-to-face familiarity of the small community and made enforcement of the peace a relatively intimate task. The burgeoning urban communities, however, pushed such informal parameters of the constabulary arrangement to the breaking point when the individuals of the city could no longer be recognized or protected as part of a close communal relationship with common values. Law enforcement agents who had previously relied on assistance from private citizens when their own resources proved inadequate found that the residents of the larger urban areas were unwilling to help.[7]

Boston in 1822 is a good example of the impending crisis over law and order. The General Court of Massachusetts allowed that such chaos could no longer be governed through the traditional town meeting. Rather,

---

[7] Roger Lane, *Policing the City—Boston, 1822–1885* (Cambridge, Mass.: Harvard University Press, 1967), p. 12.

it was proposed that the local area should be constituted a corporate municipality, much in the tradition of the English city, so as to better order and control the rapidly growing urban community. This change in the structure of Boston was in direct opposition to the revolutionary glory and symbolism attached to the old town meeting.

The creation of the first incorporated city in the state of Massachusetts, like the creation of towns previously, was effected to meet "the need for 'alterations in the present government of the police'." [8] For Noah Webster and others of that era, the term police was synonymous with

> the "entire government of a city or town," "the corporation of or body of men governing the city." At the same time it was used in the less general sense [as] "the administration of the laws and regulations of a city . . . as the police of Boston," or "[the] officer entrusted with the execution of the laws of a city." [9]

The need for change was evident and the change of communities like Boston from towns to incorporated cities was directly related to issues of the police function.

The growth of a leadership class in the colonies and later in the urban centers of the new nation is important when describing early urban politics and the practice of the peace-keeping function. These politics still reflected the disparate attitudes held by the mass of qualified voters toward the traditional leadership class. The city of Boston is a good case in point. For many years the candidates for mayor of Boston were of the class, due to advantages of wealth and privacy, that was least bothered by the increasing violence and disorder accompanying the growing pains of the city. The secure positions enjoyed by these individuals made them more sensitive to the need to hold down the tax rate than to respond to demands from the people to improve the security of the city. No serious attempt was made to reduce the prevalence of vice and riots in Boston until the 1830s. The city in the 1820s experienced only sporadic outbursts of crime by rowdy stevedores or visiting sailors. In fact, the number of cases actually reaching the courts remained rather static with no more than fifty annual felony convictions recorded per year. [10] Perhaps this limited response of the justice system to crime was determined by the nature of the population settlement, and the fact that violence was isolated from those with governmental and political power. It was assumed that only those persons willingly participating in vice and rioting suffered. In fact, Josiah Quincey, the

---

[8] Ibid., p. 3.

[9] Ibid.

[10] Ibid., p. 6.

first mayor of Boston from 1823 to 1829, pointed out as a judge that "poverty, vice, and crime" were "little else than modifications of each other. . . ." [11] Such leaders assumed a somewhat sacrosanct position with regard to the police function. The burden of crime remained a family affair in the old tradition of participatory government. Crime was seen as the result of a criminal who could be expected to come from an environment which begat drunkenness, violence, and other manifestations of an uncivil lifestyle. The victims of criminal acts were seen in the same light. Hence, the victims of crime were, by and large, precluded from bringing their plight to the attention of the city leaders.

The financial structure of the early cities contributed to the lack of concern of the politically powerful toward inefficient law enforcement. Larceny as well as law enforcement was in an early stage of development. Most of the wealth at that time existed in forms that were inconvenient to steal, and a continued poor transportation network made escape difficult.[12]

Neglect of the street-level issues of police function by the leadership class of early cities practically guaranteed that the nature of the police function in these new large cities would approximate the old constabulary process. In these larger communities, police protection was provided by wards, with each ward selecting its own constable who in turn chose his assistants and night watchmen. The disinterested position of central leaders in the city, coupled with each ward having its own police force, weakened the provision of a uniform citywide police force.

The quality of the men selected by the constables to serve on watch was less than ideal. In an effort to save money some cities continued to require all citizens to serve on the watch or to pay for a substitute. Most cities were beginning to ask their constables to hire men on a permanent basis. In either case the quality of the officers remained extremely low. Watchmen employed by the city were political appointees (usually directly owing their job to the political ward captains), and the criteria of appointment were more closely related to previous political activities than to ability.[13] Although they were hired to keep the peace, watchmen were not armed and stayed far away from areas that were notorious for violence.[14] Furthermore, the patrol function was not a pres-

---

[11] Ibid., p. 20.

[12] Ibid., p. 54.

[13] Raymond B. Fosdick, *American Police Systems* (New York: The Century Co., 1921), pp. 61-62.

[14] Roger Lane, "Urbanization and Criminal Violence in the 19th Century: Massachusetts as a Test Case," in Hugh Davis Graham and Ted Robert Gurr, *The History of Violence in America: Historical and Comparative Perspectives* (New York: Praeger, 1969), pp. 474-75.

tigious or productive activity, and watchmen were expected to work at other trades during the day.[15] The political nature of the appointments coupled with the low esteem of the job helped to insure that the watch was not especially vigilant.

The peace function was further subverted by the lack of coordination and poor communication existing in the ward-by-ward police departments. In the face of a large-scale disorder, splintered political arrangements of the city constabularies made it all but impossible to carry out the police function.[16]

Problems similar to those developing in New York, Boston, and other United States cities at this time appeared even earlier in London. In 1828 Parliament enacted a law that established a new police agency for the city of London controlled by the *national government*. The London experiment proved successful, and efforts toward reform in cities of the United States attempted to incorporate many of its provisions. Some of the vital features, however, were too radical a departure from the new-found tradition of local autonomy which was jealously guarded by the citizens of the new nation. The new city police of London were to be controlled by the national Parliament. In this country, however, it was a struggle merely to establish central control of a police department at the city level in places like Philadelphia and Boston. The first police department of a citywide nature was established by city ordinance in Philadelphia in 1833. The force was composed of 24 police officers and 120 night watchmen and was financed through the estate of a wealthy philanthropist. Even with such a financial guarantee, the city fathers became disenchanted, repealing the ordinance and disbanding the force two years later. A second attempt to organize a professional citywide police force was made in Boston in 1837, as a direct response to public outcry over a series of large-scale riots.[17] Unlike the Philadelphia experiment, the force in Boston succeeded and immediately became the archetype for many other cities which were debating the merits of professional police forces.

The major structural weakness of the Boston model was its adherence to the traditional separation of day and night patrolmen. The Boston model actually unified the numerous police forces of the old ward system, establishing in its stead two police forces within the one citywide department. Forces fashioned after the Boston experiment were riddled with conflict

---

[15] James R. Richardson, *The New York Police, from Colonial Times to 1901* (New York: Oxford University Press, 1970), p. 59.

[16] Fosdick, *American Police Systems*, p. 61. An exception was the city marshall established in the city of Boston in 1823.

[17] Lane, in Graham and Gurr, *History of Violence*, p. 473.

and competition between these two separately administered police forces.

Realizing the deleterious effects of such intradepartmental rivalry, the New York legislature passed a law in 1844 providing for the unification of all police departments in New York City. The new force, organized in 1845, consisted of 800 men who were responsible for keeping the peace during both the day and night. New York's approach to a unified police force influenced many other cities. By 1870 most of the nation's largest cities had full-time police departments; by the turn of the century, there were few urban areas without formal peace-keeping forces.

Central control of these citywide forces passed to a city official such as the chief or a commissioner, "often appointed by the mayor, sometimes with the consent of the city council and sometimes elected by the people."[18] However, such executive positions within the neophyte police organizations were often occupied by powerless figureheads. The change to a professional citywide police force, often uniformed and in some cases bearing arms, did not remove the influence of local politics and the new "leadership class" of urban politicians. In reality, the chief could do little to affect the performance of his department. He lacked the power to hire and fire his own personnel. This privilege was retained by the political power barons who used positions on the police force as patronage. Within the new police departments, existing power remained at the ward level: each ward was headed by a police captain appointed by the alderman.[19] The policemen were also appointed, and direct payment to the police captain and the ward alderman for specific jobs was not unusual.[20]

The alternative to a police force that was permeated by partisan politics was the institution of tenure for policemen. At a time when the very existence of a full-time professional police force was widely believed to be a threat to individual liberty, the suggestion of tenure for policemen excited even greater fears of official tyranny.[21] As a result politicians had no difficulty limiting policemen to terms of one, two, or four years, and frequent party changes insured that inexperienced policemen were on duty most of the time.[22]

Control of the police department became a crucial element of urban political machines. The police force not only provided the machine with

---

[18] The President's Commission on Law Enforcement and Administration of Justice, *Task Force Report: The Police* (Washington, D.C.: Government Printing Office, 1967), p. 5.

[19] Fosdick, *American Police Systems*, pp. 68-69.

[20] Carl Wittke, *The Irish in America* (Baton Rouge: Louisiana State University Press, 1956), p. 59.

[21] Richardson, *The New York Police*, p. 42.

[22] Ibid., pp. 54-55.

many patronage jobs, but its control of the election machinery, a traditional function from the time of the colonial constables, gave politicians a high degree of confidence in the outcome of balloting. Policemen stationed at the polling places frequently decided who would be allowed to vote. Since there was no independent authority to which the rejected citizen could appeal, he had no recourse to such selective action.[23]

The close relationship between police and city politicians concerned prominent citizens who believed that this relationship impaired the efficiency of the police. Most of the changes that occurred in the administrative structure of the police departments during the nineteenth century were attempts, if nominal, to reduce partisan influence, but few had the desired effect.

One early reform effort was the creation of a Board of Commissioners, used first in New York City, to appoint policemen and supervise the department. The Board of Commissioners was composed of three public officials—the mayor, the recorder, and the city judge—elected by a citywide constituency. In replacing control of the police by the common council with such a board, it was hoped that ward politics would be eliminated along with lower-class influence. The three commissioners, however, maintained their ties with ward politicians and continued to use the department for political advantage. Police supervisors hired by the board frequently complained about the continuous interference of board members with administrative matters.[24]

The innovation requiring that police boards be bipartisan was another attempt to reduce the effects of partisanship in the operation of the police department without removing it from democratic control. Reformers believed that opposing party delegates would watch over each other and prevent corruption. In practice, the appointees to bipartisan boards took their roles as party representatives seriously, using their positions for party advantage. Conflict between members of different parties sometimes existed, but frequently cooperative agreements were reached about division of the spoils.[25]

Yet another attempt at curbing political influence in city police departments was the imposition of reform through external agencies. State governments, dominated by rural interests, began to take an interest in urban police problems. The state legislature of New York in 1857 passed a law

---

[23] Edward M. Levine, *The Irish and Irish Politicians* (Notre Dame: University of Notre Dame Press, 1966), p. 122.

[24] Richardson, *The New York Police*, p. 81.

[25] Fosdick, *American Police Systems*, p. 104.

giving control of the municipal police force of New York City and several surrounding counties to the state. The people of the state controlled police activities in the city, but only the urban residents were taxed for the services. From an administrative standpoint the imposition of a municipal department controlled by an agency external to the local government made coordination difficult.[26] Politically, the impact was even more convoluted. In New York City the local government continued to maintain its own force for a number of years, and rivalry between the two police departments did not aid in keeping the peace. Furthermore, the Republican administration of the state government was as eager to use the police force to strengthen its political position in the city as the local machine had been.

Police Technology: 1880
to the Present

Police forces in the twentieth century have continued to face problems of political influence and corruption. The logistics involved in placing and routing police officers in a manner which will best deter crime and disorder have also been troublesome. The problems of supervision and service have been with police forces since the first departments were established in Boston and New York. The three basic components of these problems are (1) using the police officer as an effective and visible service agent for all persons in the neighborhoods he serves; (2) communicating to him the various needs which arise outside his immediate vicinity; and (3) supervising the police officer to insure honest and efficient execution of his professional responsibilities.

The police officer has been assigned to a specific area or beat from the beginning of the "new police" in Philadelphia, New York, and Boston in the nineteenth century. It has often been argued that the patrolman was, like a foot soldier, an extension of a paramilitary, uniformed, and armed public agency. However, there are distinctions which weaken the analogy of the efficiency of a military operation to the police function. Rubinstein describes such distinctions and attendant developmental spin-offs quite well:

> A soldier works in a group whose success is dependent upon the cooperation of the members. He is under the direct supervision of superiors who can

---

[26] Elmer D. Graper, *American Police Administration: A Handbook on Police Organization and Methods of Administration in American Cities* (New York: Macmillan, 1921), pp. 1-2.

punish him if he fails to recognize that his performance is measured by the contribution he makes to the group's work. He is also influenced by the pressure exerted on him directly by his colleagues, his buddies, who are working alongside him. The territorial strategy of policing makes the patrolman a solitary worker who is dependent mainly on his personal skills and judgment. His colleagues offer him support and information, they sometimes come to his aid, but he does not often work with them. The policeman also has an occupational interest in concealing things which he knows from others, even from his closest colleagues. Moreover, the policeman, unlike the soldier, leaves his work and his colleagues behind him at the end of each day and resumes his private life.

The effort to inspire loyalty and a sense of duty in policemen by military discipline has never worked well, although every department uses the initial training period to instill some kind of fear into the recruits and maintains a bulky book of regulations employed to threaten, punish, and dismiss the recalcitrant, the lazy, and the untrustworthy. The failure of this solution should not mask the importance of a problem which plagues every department and inspires tensions between policemen and the people they regulate. A policeman has considerable power and authority. He cannot be paid enough to assure his honesty, loyalty, and bravery. Policemen do not steal because they feel they are underpaid, nor can men be inspired to bravery and high risk simply by offering them a few dollars more.[27]

Central to the problems of patrol is keeping the patrolman mobile and honest. Mobility is an ordering of police in an effective manner to produce the best preventive strategy to combat crime. Put quite simply, the best crime deterrent is the physical presence of a police officer and the farther removed the responsible officer is from any part of his district, the less efficient the preventive nature of his service. Various strategies for preventive service have been tried, but they are simple variants on the original design of the police beat which requires a patrolman to cover his entire area in a comprehensive and uniform manner.[28]

In its early stages in the American city, the model of continuous patrol mandated that the police officer, in the absence of the sophisticated communication technology of today, walk his beat in isolation. He encountered trouble without the support of fellow officers. Hence policing was a struggle to maintain a highly personalized and resourceful style in the face of the full panoply of service demands represented on his beat. At the same time the officer had to overcome the fear which attended provi-

---

[27] Jonathan Rubinstein, *City Police* (New York: Farrar, Straus, and Giroux, 1973), pp. 12-13.

[28] Ibid., p. 14.

sion of such a specialized service in the absence of support from other law enforcement officials.

Until the establishment of the telegraph in the 1850s, coordination of and communication between the patrolmen on the beat and the district commanders and executives in the central office of the chief was conveyed through runners carrying messages from the district commander to the men and vice versa. If, for example, a riot was occurring in one sector of the city, the chief and the commanders would inform other officers by this slow process.[29]

Many police departments evolving from a ward organization to a larger district organization, which was then broken down into beats, used a detailed set of meetings to supplement communication and organization processes. In Philadelphia and Brooklyn, the district commanders met first with the chief each morning. Next they met at role call with the patrolmen. Excepting this meeting, the communication of the district captain with his men was minimal and often nonexistent.

At this juncture the formalized role of part messenger, part supervisor of the district sergeants apeared. The sergeants were responsible for making the rounds of the different beats and for setting up places where they could meet with the patrolmen at specified times. Hence the sergeants in some cities came to be known as "roundsmen." Such patterns of communication made it possible to learn more about the patrolmen and their problems on the beat. It also helped to control unprofessional practices resulting from fright or corruption. However, a patrolmen could arrange his tours so that the behavior he wanted to hide from the roundsman did not occur in the area of the arranged meeting or during the time the sergeant was in his beat territory. Consequently, the sergeant began to walk a whole tour of the beat with the patrolman or to make unscheduled appearances in the patrolman's territory.

There was no guarantee that the chief could round up the necessary number of officers to handle problems at any particular time because of these inefficient attempts at communication and control of the administration of the police function. The result was that many of the district headquarters contained large dormitories where reserve police were billeted in case of emergency. The patrolman walking his beat in a continuous pattern allowed the sophisticated criminal an orderly glimpse at the structure of law enforcement and, hence, the opportunity to commit crimes knowing, with some degree of certainty, that the patrolman was located in another section of the beat.

---

[29] Ibid. The discussion which follows is strongly influenced by Jonathan Rubinstein's chapter, "Origins."

The innovations in transportation and communication affected the administration and delivery of the police function in metropolitan areas in much the same way as they affected the growth and spread of the metropolis. The introduction of the telegraph helped to refine some of the crude practices of coordination and communication existing in earlier days. The telegraph allowed the central office of the chief to communicate with district captains using Morse code and, in turn, allowed the street-level police officers to send simple messages to the district headquarters. Using the telegraph the officer was able

> to tell his district by means of a few simple signals whether he needed an ambulance, a "slow wagon" for routine duties, or a "fast wagon" for emergencies. The wagons and horses were kept at the district stations and did not go on patrol because the telegraph system was only a one-way communication system and had no mobility.[30]

The telegraph improved communication with the street. The officer was now able to send messages to the district headquarters, but the communication was one-way as the headquarters staff remained unable to contact a patrolman walking his beat. Hence the costly auxiliary force billeted at the station house was still necessary.

The invention of the telephone in the 1880s facilitated two-way communication between street-level patrolmen and headquarters. The police officer could call in to the station house from the call box and receive instructions. In some cities the police officer was required to call in every hour in order to control his behavior and keep him in contact with the district. The responsibility to call in was still up to the patrolman and if he were away from his box or did not care to call he remained unavailable to calls from the district office. Horns, lights, double signals, and other mechanisms were installed on call boxes in an effort to obtain the attention of the beat patrolman. These gadgets were subject to problems: horns and lights merged with the pandemonium of city streets and were often unnoticed by the patrolman, sometimes attracting an interested crowd of citizens instead. Gadgetry unfortunately often resulted in more confusion than communication.[31]

The patrolman could still control to a great extent whether or not he would be "found" by his supervisor. In fact, the process of supervision

---

[30] Ibid., p. 16. See also V. A. Leonard, *Police Communication Systems* (Berkeley, Calif.: University of California Press, 1938), chapter I. Rubinstein also cites James McCague, *The Second Rebellion: The New York City Draft Riots of 1863* (New York: Dial Press, 1968), as an excellent source on the use of the telegraph in police departments.

[31] Ibid.

of the beat officer was conceived as a game of finding the officer for the supervisor. Walking a straight beat so that the officer could be seen from any direction on a street or allowing the officer to have legitimate hiding places such as a barber's chair where he could rest and still be observed and observe the street were among many patterns which were tried. Sergeants might show up early and observe the direction from which an officer approached a scheduled meeting place. The sergeant could backtrack from the direction of the officer's approach and discover the place where he was hiding. The administrative problems of supervision to insure honest public service remained despite the innovations in service supplied by the use of the telephone.

The introduction of the patrol car and the two-way radio in the early years of the twentieth century went a long way toward curing some of the ills of police performance. Many heralded the invention of the automobile as the dawn of a new era in policing. The police officer could now patrol a much larger beat with speed and efficiency. He could be observed by a cruising supervisor at any time, and the automobile kept him inside and away from the elements, removing his need to hide out somewhere. August Vollmer, one of the foremost police administrators and reformers, argued that

> with the advent of the radio equipped car a new era has come . . . . Districts of many square miles . . . are now covered by the roving patrol car, fast, efficient, stealthy, having no regular beat to patrol, just as liable to be within 60 feet as 3 miles of the crook plying his trade—the very enigma of this specialized fellow who is coming to realize now that a few moments may bring them down about him like a swarm of bees—this lightning swift "angel of death." [32]

The popularity of such "angels of death" is discussed in the President's Commission Task Force on Science and Technology. In 1930, at the time of Vollmer's assessment, there were less than 1,000 police cars in the country and only the city of Detroit employed radio cars. Two decades later, there were over 5,000 police radio transmitters in the United States and, by 1966, there were over 200,000 police radio cars in operation.[33] In addition to the radio and the automobile, a variety of instruments of

---

[32] Cited by Rubinstein as originally suggested in the Wickersham Commission, the National Commission on Law Observance and Enforcement, Report No. 15, *The Police* (Washington, D.C.: Government Printing Office, 1930), pp. 90-98.

[33] The President's Commission on Law Enforcement and the Administration of Justice, *Task Force Report: Science and Technology* (Washington, D.C.: Government Printing Office, 1967), pp. 116, 143-56.

communication and detection now exist. Among them are the walkie-talkie and various radar devices including radar cars as well as radar hand guns to detect speeders.

With the advent of both the car and communication devices which improved supervision of the police and the accompanying professionalization of many police forces has come a certain decrease in political influence on the police. Hence, the police have been able to redraw service territories along lines which are best served by expanding technologies rather than political wards which service political interests. However, as later chapters in this book will suggest, while such technology did succeed in significantly upgrading police service, the problems of supervision, political meddling, police morale, and efficient public service are still dramatically evident.

Commissions, Reform, and the Age-Old Issues

In the early years of the twentieth century the nation at last appeared to take seriously the notion of reform of the politically influenced urban and metropolitan police department. Even with the technological advances in patrol service, the twentieth century has seen literally hundreds of public commissions on law enforcement cry out for reform. In 1931 the famous Wickersham Commission decided that the term of the police officer was too short, communication in urban areas of over 300,000 was woefully inadequate, and equipment provided police departments was tragically limited. The Commission also underscored the continuing reliance of the average police officer upon political officials for the long-term security of his job. Moreover, as far back as the 1920s, the Missouri Crime Commission pointed out that in the average American city the average police officer was expected to be familiar with and uphold 30,000 federal, state, and local laws.[34]

The political influence, the complexity of the job, and the inadequacies of both technology and training became the evident problems of police in the first half of the twentieth century. The Wickersham Commission, the myriad of State Crime Commissions like the Missouri Commission, local reform groups, and the recent Presidential Task Forces and commissions on crime and administration of justice and law enforcement are all representatives of organizations whose mounting demands for reform con-

---

[34] President's Commission, *Task Force Report: The Police*, p. 7.

tinue to mirror the basic questions that first forced communities to set up the peace-keeping function. At question are:

1. the nature of the police function;
2. the proper technology for administering and supporting the servicing of the police function;
3. the reforms necessary to limit or eliminate political intrusions and corruption.

PART II

Definitions and
Caricatures

Definitions: Academic Perspectives on the Police Function   3

As with any phenomenon rich with violent reality an attempt to define the police service will be elusive; while such a definition intends to provide a comprehensive description of police service, it will always remain remote and only partially accurate. In the previous chapters the history of the development of police service in metropolitan areas has been outlined. However, no firm definition of the police service (or the police function) has been provided.

The basic conceptualizations of the police function reviewed in this chapter are all less than complete definitions. Ideally, a definition is a conceptualization of a phenomenon which sets limits upon its identity in a manner which identifies the phenomenon in an objective and nondebatable way. In its written form therefore it becomes a "definitive" statement which so encapsulates the nature of the phenomenon that most persons will agree upon the definition.

Such a definition of the police function in metropolitan America has eluded both scholars and governmental officials. The descriptions we will discuss have been considered "definitions" by those proposing them. Inasmuch as they do fulfill the qualities of a definition through the setting of limits of discussion about the police function they are definitional in nature. But since they are often open to legitimate disagreement from proponents of other definitional approaches, they remain, at most, partial definitions of the police function and, at least, merely categoric descriptions of some facets of police behavior or the police function. In short, they are more descriptions of selected characteristics of law enforcement or perspectives from which to justify the police than they are definitions of the police function. The myriad of descriptive categories which are provided confounds analysis of the law enforcement function. Some practitioners and scholars are content to detail specific tasks of a patrolman or a detective and not consider anything more than the job description to be the definition. Others are so concerned with a comprehensive description of the police function that they present definitions which are so general and amorphous that they belie concrete application. The definition of the police function seems to fluctuate depending on the concerns of those attempting to define it: some scholars are concerned with the duties of the individual police officer; some with justifying the presence of the police; and others with detailing the bureaucratic role of the police.

The most common conceptualization of the police function today is primarily concerned with examining the day-to-day behavior of the police officer as he goes about the execution of the duties of law enforcement and order maintenance.[1] Almost as popular are arguments which attempt to justify the presence of the police officer and his various practices as the primary agent of social control in urban society.[2]

A less popular variation is the "bureaucratic-link" description of the police: the police officer is defined as the extension of public authority in an attempt to explain his role as part of the centralized legal and political authority of the state.[3] Other scholars in this category characterize the police officer as a street-level bureaucrat,[4] describing his role from the position of the clientele and the external and decentralized demands of the clientele. In each case, the definition of the police function relies on description of the bureaucratic duties of the public police officer and justification of his role as the link between the citizenry and the public authority of the state.

---

[1] James Q. Wilson, *Varieties of Police Behavior: The Management of Law and Order in Eight Communities* (Cambridge, Mass.: MIT Press, 1968); Michael Banton, *The Policeman and the Community* (New York: Basic Books, 1964); Jerome Skolnick, *Justice Without Trial: Law Enforcement in a Democratic Society* (New York: John Wiley, 1967).

[2] For a discussion of this approach see Harlan Hahn, "The Public and the Police," in *Police in Urban Society*, ed. Harlan Hahn (Beverly Hills: SAGE Publications, 1971), pp. 9-33. The basic approach of this chapter is informed by the approach Hahn uses in this essay.

[3] Ibid., pp. 22-26.

[4] Michael Lipsky, "Street-Level Bureaucracy and the Analysis of Urban Reform," *Urban Affairs Quarterly* 6, no. 4 (June): 391-409.

The history of the police function in the United States has been the history of a nation's confusion over how to police itself. It is understandable that scholars and practitioners are presently having difficulty arriving at a definition of the police function which will satisfy each one of them. More than one observer has reviewed discussions of the police function, or the trials and failures of one city after another in attempting to provide satisfactory and acceptable service, and argued that more than a question of proper technology and proper staffing is involved.[5] The questions a metropolitan nation has yet to answer are: What is it we want the police to do? How is it that we want our lives protected yet undisturbed in the name of such protection?

The Special Nature of the Police Function

It is part of the reality and mythology of society-building to assume that factors such as law and order, authority and justice, provide the foundation for the society's continued maintenance and well-being. Such factors are assumed to be fundamental in guiding the individual social conduct of a citizenry. As detailed in chapter 1, more than any other public servant, the police officer is an extension of the authority of the state, an executor of laws in the name of social order, and the provider of social justice. The nature of the police function incurs a wide range of duties and a set of expectations approaching sacredness.

Police officers can be expected to play an important part in linking the average citizen with awesome tenets which sustain society, yet affect the individual only remotely. At the same time, the police officer is expected to respond to diverse human needs and styles of living that are purely ordinary. Finally, in order to accomplish both the awesome and mundane features of his task the police officer is provided a most divergent range of professional tools (from a good pair of walking shoes to a gun) and professional directives (from the most elegantly worded law to the order, "Stop or I will shoot!"). In such a milieu, to define the police function exclusively in terms of duties or bureaucratic-linkage or solely as an agent of social control would be short-sighted and incomplete. None of these approaches to the study of police in metropolitan areas is

---

[5] James Q. Wilson, "Dilemmas of Police Administration," *Public Administration Review* 28, no. 5 (September-October 1968): 407-16; A. J. Reiss, "Public Perceptions and Recollections About Crime, Law Enforcement, and Criminal Justice," *Studies in Crime and Law Enforcement in Major Metropolitan Areas*, vol. I (Washington, D.C.: Government Printing Office, 1967).

definitely all-inclusive, and none is mutually exclusive. However, taken as a composite, these definitions are worthy of extensive examination.

Social Control

One of the most common ways of describing the police officer has been as an "agent of social control." This loose conceptualization seems to satisfy the requirements of definition and, for many, to provide a justification for the police function. Such a description of the police officer is used more often by practitioners and the popular press than by scholars because it does provide a colorful and substantial justificatory focus. However, some scholars utilize the social control approach to the police function.[6] William Westley, for example, argues that the police function is part of the structural network of controls which binds society and orders the individual and the group.[7] He borrows this structure-of-controls approach from Simmel[8] and points out that

> the structure of control that regulates the conduct of the members of a society or social group . . . [occurs] . . . on three levels: the societal, as embodied in the law; the group, as embodied in custom; and the individual, as embodied in conscience or morality.[9]

Such an ordering of controls causes many to include the police agent under the heading of social control. Inasmuch as we exert our own personal controls upon ourselves through the invoking of the boundaries of our conscience and the moral decisions which provide order and predictability in our everyday life, we find that social control within the larger society and for the protection of ourselves is an understanble and justifiable utilization of some public servants.

Harlan Hahn uses a Simmelian-like concept when he points to a second type of control which he prefers to call "social conventions." This concept is very similar to the concept of group mores. In fact, Hahn defines social conventions as "those rules (which) may include established traditions, as well as norms or mores."[10] There is little doubt that the informal

---

[6] William A. Westley, *Violence and the Police: A Sociological Study of Law, Custom, and Morality* (Cambridge, Mass.: MIT Press, 1970).

[7] Ibid.

[8] George Simmel, *The Sociology of George Simmel*, trans. Kurt Wolff (Glencoe, Ill.: The Pree Press, 1950).

[9] Westley, *Violence and the Police*, pp. 8-9.

[10] Hahn, in *Police in Urban Society*, p.13.

associational patterns of groups have impacts on the social conduct of individuals and significantly affect the order of society.

With such a rich and varied tradition for experiencing control, it is small wonder that the average citizen encountering the boundaries of his conscience, the controls of his job, the controls of ethnic, neighborhood and other groups finds it satisfying to consider the police officer as a type of agent of social control, although such a term may not be part of the citizen's everyday vocabulary. The police officer is the administrator of the formal regulations which result from political decisions of the public authority of the State. Also, quite importantly, the police officer, as suggested by the definition "agent of social control," stands as an emissary—a representative or an *agent* of the political definitions of order. Hence, constant experiences with personal and group controls make such a definition of the police officer and his function quite understandable.

This view of the police officer as the emissary of social control as practiced by the dominant society is stated in a more ominous way by Joseph Lohman, dean of the School of Criminology of the University of California at Berkeley: "[t]he police function [is] to support and enforce the interests of the dominant political, social, and economic interests of the town, and only incidentally to enforce the law." [11] In addition to being an administrator of the law then, the policeman is also the representative of the dominant interests of the society.

The role as emissary of the dominant society and as an agent whose prime administrative task is to enforce the laws of the dominant society will inevitably be discordant with the individual life-styles, customs, ethnic identities, and even the political definitions of society found in the diverse groups of the metropolis. While the definition of the police officer as the agent of social control seems straightforward and comprehensive, strict adherence to such a definition shows this view of the police as culture bound and predictive of basic conflicts between the agent of social control role and the diverse social and political enclaves which make up contemporary metropolitanism.

Law and Order

Another of the more popular conceptions of the police role is the law and order function. Often the law function and the order function are separated in a manner which produces distinct and often conflicting roles for the police officer. The police officer's job is often described as one

---

[11] Westley, *Violence and the Police*, p. 16.

of *enforcing the law* on the one hand and *maintaining the order* on the other.[12]

Two students[13] of the police service approach the distinction between law enforcement and order maintenance in much the same way: they believe there are policemen who are by and large law enforcement officers (such as detectives and traffic officers), and others who are by and large responsible for maintaining order (the beat patrolmen). Michael Banton terms the former "law officers" and the latter "peace officers." [14] James Wilson states that

> policy making for the police is complicated by the fact that, at least in large cities, the police department is an organization with at least two objectives, one of which produces conflict and the other of which cannot be obtained. . . . The first objective I call *order maintenance*—the handling of disputes, or behavior which threatens to produce disputes, among persons who disagree over the assignment of blame for what is agreed to be wrong or unseemly conduct. . . . The second objective is *law enforcement*—the application of legal sanctions, usually by means of an arrest, to persons who injure or deprive innocent victims.[15]

Sociologist Jerome Skolnick approaches this conceptualization of the police function differently from Wilson in his discussion of police behavior.[16] First, Skolnick alludes to the fact that the literature concerning police prior to the work of contemporary scholars was, like all studies in this field, concerned with description and reform. However, recent scholarly efforts interested in police have begun to deal with the theories or philosophies of policing.[17] Skolnick quotes Fosdick who wrote, in the

---

[12] See Wilson, *Varieties of Police Behavior;* Banton, *The Policeman and the Community;* and Skolnick, *Justice Without Trial,* to name a few studies which start from this perspective.

[13] Wilson, ibid. See also James Q. Wilson, "Dilemmas of Police Administration," cited earlier, and Banton, ibid.

[14] Banton, *The Policeman and the Community,* pp. 6-7.

[15] Wilson, "Dilemmas of Police Administration," p. 407. See also Wilson, *Varieties of Police Behavior,* chapter 1. Others who have made similar distinctions are Egon Bittner, "The Police on Skid Row: A Study of Peace Keeping," *American Sociological Review* 32 (October 1967): 699-715; Eugene Wenninger and John P. Clark take on a very Parsonian image with a distinction between "value maintenance" (law enforcement) and "goal attainment" (close to Parson's "pattern maintenance" or order maintenance in a Wilson sense) in their work, "A Theoretical Orientation for Police Studies," in *Juvenile Gangs in Context,* ed. Malcolm W. Klein (Englewood Cliffs: Prentice Hall, 1956), pp. 161-72.

[16] Skolnick, *Justice Without Trial.*

[17] Ibid., pp. 3-6.

characteristic fashion of early police scholars, "[we] are concerned with facts and conditions and not with theories or labels." [18]

For Skolnick, the theoretical description of police behavior in the United States is centered around the conflict between order and legality. Skolnick recognizes (as do Wilson and others) the fact that the " . . . common juxtaposition of 'law and order' is an oversimplification. Law is not merely an instrument of order, but may frequently be an adversary." [19] However, Skolnick moves beyond the more classic distinction [20] of Wilson and Banton to the concepts of order and legality. Doig puts this distinction very well:

> Skolnick is concerned mainly with the conflict between two goals that might guide police behavior. One is adherence to the role of law, i.e., police attitudes and actions which place high priority on the rights of individual citizens and on legal restraints upon governmental officials. The second objective is managerial efficiency: the goal of maintaining order (controlling criminal behavior) with an efficient, technologically sophisticated police organization. [21]

Thus for Skolnick the concept of order examplifies a bureaucratic drive for efficiency and the traditional American emphasis on organizational effectiveness. This approach to the discretionary functions attached to initiative in bureaucracy is ostensibly different from the intellectual approach of scholars such as Wilson and Banton, who discuss the entire gestalt of the order maintenance function.

Rising from this theoretical underpinning is the stated purpose of the Skolnick study:

> The police in a democratic society are required to maintain order and to do so under the rule of law. As functionaries charged with maintaining order, they are part of the bureaucracy. The ideology of democratic bureaucracy emphasizes initiative rather than disciplined adherence to rules and regulations. By contrast, the rule of law emphasizes the rights of individual citizens and constraints upon the initiative of legal officials. This tension between the operational consequences of ideas of order efficiency and initia-

---

[18] Ibid., p. 4, as found in Raymond Fosdick, *American Police Systems* (New York: The Century Company, 1920), p. 221. Skolnick also cites such scholars and practitioners as William H. Parker and O. W. Wilson as examples of the theory-void treatments of the past.

[19] Ibid., p. 7.

[20] See such criminology sources as Harry Elmer Barnes and Negley K. Teeters, *New Horizons in Criminology* (New York: Prentice-Hall, 1951); Norval Morris, *The Habitual Criminal* (Cambridge, Mass.: Harvard Press, 1951); and in particular, Sheldon Glueck, *Crime and Correction: Selected Papers* (Cambridge, Mass.: Addison-Wesley, 1952).

[21] Jameson W. Doig, "Police Problems and Proposals, and Strategies for Change," *Public Administration Review* 28, no. 5 (September-October 1968): 394.

tive, on the one hand, and legality, on the other, constitutes the principle problem of police as a democratic legal organization.[22]

Skolnick, Wilson, and Banton offer three different interpretations of the distinction between law enforcement and order maintenance. For Banton, the distinction between the law enforcement function and the order maintenance function is found in bureaucratic distinctions between the law enforcers of the department, such as the detectives or the traffic officers, and the order maintainers of the department, or the "peace officers" who walk the beat in uniform. Banton is more concerned with the *nature of the job* within the bureaucracy, while Wilson is more concerned with the *nature of the offense* addressed by the bureaucracy: order maintenance offenses are those which cause disorder during a dispute or threat of a dispute; and law enforcement demands are those which demand the application of a specific legal sanction (such as arrest) for a specifically defined offense against another, resulting in injury or some other specific deprivation. While Skolnick and Wilson use the same basic distinction when discussing the various functionaries within the police department, they take decidedly different views of interrelations of the law and order dichotomy.

Skolnick is concerned with the operationalization of the law and order functions of police as members of a democratic legal organization. He sees law and order as different functions as the result of the very dependence that a democratic society must place upon the principle of legality. This principle subordinates the rules and procedures of order maintenance to the strict due process requirements of the law. As such the law protects the citizens from arbitrary or totalitarian executive directives to place the citizens in jail for some spurious act of nonconformity. Legal scholar Stanford H. Kadish puts the relationship of order to the law in rather specific terms:

> The principle of *nulla poena sine lege* [no punishment without law] imposes formidable restraints upon the definition of criminal conduct. Standards of conduct must meet stringent tests of specificity and clarity, may act only prospectively, and must be strictly construed in favor of the accused. Further, the definition of criminal conduct has largely come to be regarded as a legislative function, thereby precluding the judiciary from devising new crimes. The public-mischief doctrine and the sometimes over-generalized "ends" of criminal conspiracy are usually regarded as anomalous departures from this main stream. The cognate principle of procedural regularity and fairness, in short, due process of law, commands that the legal standard be applied to the individual with scrupulous fairness in order to minimize the chances of convicting the innocent, protect against abuse of official

---

[22] Skolnick, *Justice Without Trial*, p. 6.

power, and generate an atmosphere of impartial justice. As a consequence, a complex network of procedural requirements embodied variously in constitutional, statutory, or judge-made law is imposed upon the criminal adjudicatory process—public trial, unbiased tribunal, legal representation, open hearing, confrontation, and related concomitants of procedural justice.[23]

It is important to remember that scholars like Skolnick and Kadish are arguing that the law possesses a superordinate position to the principle of social order. The principle of legality as found in the administration of the rule of law protects the citizen and the group from those arbitrary or capricious acts of both legislators and administrators who would quite blindly impose their own mores and morality upon the different group and individual customs. Inasmuch as the law is composed of such procedural regulations on the behavior of public officials, it is superior to the function of maintaining the social order, hence different from and in conflict with complete adherence to such order. At the same time, the law is substantive as well as procedural. Here the substantive crimes delineated by the rules of law are at times compatible with the maintenance of order, inasmuch as they delineate specific acts which can be construed as disorderly.

The police function is composed of law enforcement functions which are procedural and substantive, and of order maintenance functions which are to be found formally spelled out within the law and informally relegated to the patrolman. The role of the police officer is frustrated as well as aided by the mixture of conflict and compatibility between the law enforcement function and the order maintenance task. He is aided by the substantive delineation of laws which dictate the nature of a crime and make his task of identification of criminals easier. He is also aided by the broad discretion he has at his disposal for such crimes as disorderly conduct which gives him the latitude to remove from the streets a suspect he feels is dangerous and participating in activities which serve as preconditions of criminality. On the other hand, the patrolman is frustrated by the procedural regulations to which he must continually adhere in order to protect the rights of the accused. From the *Miranda* card to interrogation procedures, wire-tapping, and procurement of a warrant, police officers and the detectives, in particular, often feel that too much attention is given the rights of the accused and too little attention is being paid to the rising crime rates and mounting frustration of police officers facing the increasing sophistication of criminals. Such frustration invites the criticism that there is too much concern for the procedural protections and too little concern for the police officer as an agent of social control and a crime stopper.

---

[23] Stanford H. Kadish, "Legal Norm and Discretion in the Police and Sentencing Process," *Harvard Law Review* 75 (1962): 904-5.

An Arm of Public Authority

The phrase "long arm of the law" is a common one, often used to describe the ever-present possibility that a police officer is just around the corner if a person dares to speed, or drink too much, or commit a more serious offense. A rather new definition of the police function incorporates more than the threat of punishment. One proponent of this approach, Harlan Hahn, argues that:

> Fundamentally, police functions seem to comprise an *extension of political authority*. Political decisions concerning basic regulations of public behavior eventually are transmitted from executive, legislative, and judicial bodies through policemen to the public. Law enforcement officers, therefore, constitute the extended arm of the polity and a crucial link between ordinary social conduct and the rules devised by duly constituted public officials. In fact, policemen may be the principal representatives of public authority at the grassroots level.[24]

This approach to the police function argues that the source of legitimacy or efficacy of the actions of the police officer on the street is the authority of the State. Thus, this role of the police officer is accepted only to the extent that the citizens accept the right of public officials of the State to legitimately command a populace. Inherent in this argument are three basic premises of public authority: (1) the right of command; (2) the legitimacy of public institutions; and (3) the acceptance of public authority by the citizens.

First and foremost a government will possess public authority only if it possesses recognized sovereignty. Such sovereignty extends to all the territory under the government's jurisdiction, and over the residents of such territory as well. The right to command through the dictates of governmentally promulgated law is part of the sovereign character of public authority. Weber has extended such sovereignty to its most fundamental roots. In the case of a breach of either the territorial or legal sovereignty of the public government, the ultimate legitimacy of the State as a sovereign resides in its nature as a "human community that (successfully) claims the *monopoly of the legitimate use of physical force* within a given territory" [25] and uses such force as a sanction, real or implied, against any breach of public order.

---

[24] Hahn, in *Police in Urban Society*, p. 23. Emphasis added.

[25] Max Weber, "Politics as a Vocation," *From Max Weber*, ed. H. H. Gerth and C. W. Mills (New York: Oxford University Press, 1958), as quoted in Joe R. Feagin, "Home Defense and the Police," *Police in Urban Society*, ed. Harlan Hahn (Beverly Hills: SAGE Publications, 1971), pp. 101-18.

Second, it is argued by adherents of this approach that the source of legitimacy of public authority resides in the legitimacy of public institutions. To this end Hahn argues:

> Not only must a government possess the capability of formulating and enforcing laws for the residents who live within its borders, but the ability to issue and impose those rules also must be perceived as justifiable and acceptable. The capacity of police officers, as agents of the government, to administer the laws may be determined by public assessments of the moral rectitude of executive, legislative, and judicial institutions. If a prevalent belief develops among the citizenry that political bodies lack the appropriate credentials for enacting legislation, then the propriety of police officers, acting in behalf of the state, in enforcing those laws might be seriously questioned. Police powers, therefore, are closely related to public appraisals of political legitimacy.[26]

Inasmuch as police activity is closely related to public appraisals of the political legitimacy of the State, the consequences of such reliance are mixed for the police officer. On the one hand, actions of the police can be more readily accepted when *carried out in the name of the sovereign state.* The sanctity of such a mantle of legitimacy will make the actions of the police officer most acceptable. On the other hand, the police officer can encounter groups of individuals who hold no great respect for certain laws of the State, for certain policy pronouncements, or for the government of the State in its entirety. When legitimacy of the State is in doubt for one reason or another, the potential for a less-than-receptive environment for police service is high. Hence the types of criticisms logged against the State in general can be easily transferred to the police officer as the extension of public authority is street-level bureaucracy. Michael Lipsky describes the police officer as one who, through his actions, can either reap citizen support or criticism for the system. Lipsky argues:

> In American cities today, police officers, teachers, and welfare workers are under siege. Their critics variously charge them with being insensitive, unprepared to work with ghetto residents, incompetent, resistant to change and racist. These accusations, directed toward individuals, are transferred to the bureaucracies in which they work.[27]

Whether the pattern of citizen dissatisfaction with police behavior is the result of that actual dissatisfaction and thus is transferred to the central

---

[26] Hahn, in *Police in Urban Society,* p. 24.

[27] Lipsky, "Street-Level Bureaucracy," p. 391.

bureaucracy and other elements of the political system, or whether citizen dissatisfaction with police presence is indicative of citizen dissatisfaction with the political system is an interesting but hollow question. The answer will rarely be exclusively one or the other: the police function will be perceived as satisfactory or unsatisfactory most probably through a mixture of system and service satisfactions. It is crucial to emphasize that police officers are the uniformed embodiment of the State. They are the street-level bureaucrats, since they represent the law enforcement bureaucracy to the average citizen. Conversely the citizens' satisfaction with police behavior will be influenced by their perception of the State.

Definitions in Retrospect

Contrary to what some scholars might argue, the previous conceptions of the police function do not represent conflicting definitions. When used in proper juxtaposition to each other they are complementary rather than conflicting. However, none of them are, in and of themselves, sufficient definitions of the police function. The conception of the police officer as an agent of social control alone is broad and open to a highly skewed and repressive interpretation of the function. However, to argue that the police function is not, in part, a social control activity would be inaccurate.

At the same time the general bifurcation of the duties of the police officer into law enforcement functions and order maintenance activities is a necessary but insufficient description of the police function. While such a delineation of police duties is a helpful descriptive technique, it is not comprehensive inasmuch as the thrust of this approach is concerned with *what* the police *do*, not *who* the police officer is or *what* the police officer represents.

Finally, another necessary description, yet insufficient definition, of the police function is that of the police officer as an extension of the political and public authority of the State. The police officer is the front-line or street-level representative of the sovereign political authority of the State. Not only are his behavior patterns cloaked in the sanctity of the State, but they are also influenced by the extent to which the State and its various legislative and administrative dictates are accepted by the citizenry. As such the street-level role of the police officer can be just as important as the decisions of the upper-level bureaucrat to service success. Further, the actions of the street-level bureaucrat can also affect the public's attitude toward the bureaucracy which the police officer represents. This definition of the arm of the public trust has the advantage of confronting the questions of *who* are police and *what* do they represent, but it takes little specific account of the duties of the police officer and the conflicting nature of those duties generally specified under the headings of law enforcement and order maintenance.

There are several facets to the police function or, alternatively, there are several police functions, depending on whether the purpose of the definition is to outline the duties, the goals, or the representativeness of the police. For example, using the law enforcement-order maintenance description, a great deal can be learned about the conflict and congruence such duties create for the police officer on the beat. Further, such definitional criteria help clarify the distinctions between different types of police officers, traffic patrol, detectives, and beat patrolmen.

In conclusion, a commonly acceptable and totally comprehensive definition of the police function continues to elude scholars and practitioners alike. An effort at comprehensiveness is made in table 3-1. Again, it should be pointed out that these descriptive qualities of the police function are not accurate in any particular case. They are simply an attempt to catalogue and characterize as best we can the various faces of the police function. Further, we are arguing that various definitions of the police function which, in the past, have been applied by scholars to the police in some exclusive manner are each, by themselves, insufficient. Such definitions address different questions and while they might answer one of the questions about the police function accurately, they fail to meet the test of other questions (table 3-1).

TABLE 3-1

Police Function

Definitional Queries	Descriptive Quality
Who	Street-level bureaucrats Agents of social control
What/How	Law enforcement Order maintenance
Where/When	Street-level (direct contact with the citizenry—24 hours a day)
Why	Extension of political authority in order to preserve the State

Caricatures: Citizen Perceptions of the Police Function

4

Street-Level View of the Police Function

While the partial definitions treated in the last chapter form an important baseline for this discussion of the police function in the metropolis, it would be presumptuous to assume that citizens, in everyday life, discuss the police officer in the same measured terms. Such conceptualizations may seem reasonable from a scholarly vantage point, but the views of the police function from the street are often more reflective of the basic problems of policing than of the more ethereal societal goals of order and legality.

Street-level caricatures (a more accurate term than definition) of the police function seem to produce images of a police officer which are, on the one hand, hostile and nonsupportive, and, on the other, varying from highly supportive to apathetic. For some, the police officer is identified as "Dick Tracy . . . crime stopper." Support for such crime stoppers is most often observed in the bumper stickers and buttons of "support your local police." For others, the police officer is part of an oppressive army which catalyzes disorder and riots rather than preserves order. Still, for others, the mention of the police function brings to mind an image of racists who provide racially-motivated differentials in service to white, black, and brown communities. The police officer is often seen as a patsy who accepts bribes and as a flunky for the political powers both inside and outside of city hall. In short, such street-level views of the police officer, if not totally removed from the antiseptic definitions of the last chapter, are at least expressed in very different words.

At the street level no other public servant catalyzes, at once, as much support and criticism from the citizens as the police officer. He is the brunt of a litany of caricatures used to catalogue hostility and stereotyping. Whatever the reasons for such basically negative caricatures, most of them have persisted since the first urban police forces were formally created in the early and mid-1800s. Now, as then, the most popular conceptions of the police are very likely to be negative ones that center around rather specific social problems. Such basic issues as urban rioting; ethnic and racial diversity and hostility; increasing crime rates; fragmented and overlapping police jurisdictions and inconsistent patterns of funding, training, and equipment provision; allegations of police brutality and police corruption; and inconsistent patterns of service are all significant reasons for many of the prevailing negative caricatures and the stereotypes which abound when police are discussed.

Further, such popularly espoused caricatures and complaints of police service in metropolitan areas serve not only as distinguishing features of the public view of modern police policy but also as important indicators of metropolitan growth. The image of the police officer as the crime stopper and the converse dilemma of rising crime rates fosters the image of the dumb gumshoe who is continually outwitted and unable to deal with the rise in crime. Yet, such increase in crime is a manifestation of the increased heterogeneity (diversity) of the metropolitan phenomenon: most of the increase in crime has been in the central cities, adding further evidence to the conception of the central city as a place of high-cost citizenry demanding high levels of service and living in basically undesirable subcommunities as compared to the burgeoning suburbs. The patterns of racial spread and diversity in the metropolis have been accompanied by an increase in political violence and complaints about racially insensitive police service, police brutality, and inconsistent patterns of service and corruption.

At the same time, metropolitan patterns of governmental and economic spread and diversity have been accompanied by significant fragmentation and overlapping of police jurisdictions and inconsistent patterns of funding, training, and equipment provision. These complaints and caricatures of the police function at the street level are representative of an alternative set of definitions of police service and serve as a set of baselines from which to discuss the growth of metropolitanism. Such caricatures reflect a view of the redistribution of people and economic activity of metro-politanism in terms of the various issues which surround the police function. Economic spread and diversity can be reflected in the fundamental problems of providing the tax base necessary to support increased salaries, better training, and more substantial and professional equipment for police.

In many of our metropolitan areas, the history of corruption in local government is often a chronicle of political intrusion into the police department. The concomitant growth of local governmental reform is, at the same time, the measure of the growth of various types of governmental reform in police departments as well. Thus, this street-level view of police is helpful when studying government in the metropolis.

Crime and Crimefighters in Metropolitan Areas

Perhaps the most common view of the police officer is that of a crime-fighter. The police officer and the duties he is asked to perform have been perceived in romantic fashion by innumerable chroniclers, writers, and entertainers through the years. From the medieval balladeer to the earliest newspaper reporters, the adventures of police and their violent brushes with crime have made for good tales and good copy. However,

> this exploitation of policemen has not been confined to hack writers and police reporters. Daniel Defoe, Henry Fielding (who was also a police magistrate), Honoré de Balzac, and Charles Dickens profited greatly from listening to famous policemen of their times telling "war stories." (Dickens used his connections with the police to take guided tours of London's and New York's underworlds.) But for them too, as for the reporter and the script writer, policemen were adventurers into dark places rather than workers on the city's streets.[1]

The average television viewer can hardly turn on the set at night without finding some dramatic violence being investigated by a police officer or a private detective who has just retired from a police force. The prime-time network view of the police function is one in which the average police officer will, in thirty to ninety minutes, solve a murder, a rape, or a major robbery, or quell a case of collective violence and the like. While such excursions into the romantically violent undergrowth of American urban crime often make for extremely good Nielsen ratings, they also extend the age-old preoccupation of the public and the press with the dramatic

---

[1] Jonathan Rubinstein, *City Police* (New York: Farrar, Straus and Giroux, 1973), p. ix.

side of the police function, the investigation of violent crimes against persons or large and costly crimes against property. Script writers and police reporters are constrained by the nature of their tasks to describe those facets of the police function which touch upon the macabre, the unusual, the dramatic, or the sensational. Thus, they ignore the larger portion of the police officer's job, which is more than crimefighting and which is oftentimes much less exciting.

Crime as the
Basic Measure of
Police Effectiveness

Perhaps it is a carry-over from the old "war story" mentality or perhaps it is that crimes are the handiest measure of "production," but in any case, the rates of violent and dramatic crimes against property and persons are most often used to indicate the success of police policy at the local as well as the national level. As the statistics and headlines have catalogued a rising crime rate in the past few years, so too have the politicians called for stronger law enforcement policy. The public has responded with heightened fear of crime.

The level of public anxiety over the *apparent* increase in crime in the past few years is substantial. In 1967, the President's Commission on Law Enforcement and the Administration of Justice reported that crime was the second highest domestic concern of Americans. Only a year later, a Gallup poll found that Americans ranked crime as the most serious domestic problem. In fact, a study of residents in high crime areas of Chicago and Boston points to an increasing urban pattern of paranoia over crime. "Because of their fear of crime, 43 percent of those answering said they stay off the streets at night; 35 percent said they do not speak to strangers; 21 percent said they use cars and cabs at night; and 20 percent said they would like to move to another neighborhood." [2] There is little doubt that there has been a real increase in crime, using the Uniform Crime Reports of the Federal Bureau of Investigation as the basic source of all figures on crime rates in the metropolitan areas of this country. However, it is not at all clear which crimes are the most numerous and hence should be the real source of the public concern. Using the FBI data, table 4-1 demonstrates that the increase in crimes which are reported to the FBI has been nothing short of spectacular. Although these are the

---

[2] President's Commission on Law Enforcement and the Administration of Justice, as cited in *U.S. News and World Report, Crime in America: Causes and Cures* (Washington, D.C.: Books by *U.S. News and World Report*, 1972), p. 14.

TABLE 4-1

Offenses Known to Police in Cities

	1935	1940	1945	1950	1955	1960	1965	1970	1971
Criminal homicide									
Murder	3,423	3,509	3,711	3,467	3,676	4,321	6,180	11,264	12,607
Manslaughter	2,967	2,768	2,966	2,288	2,580	2,922	3,907	4,402	4,401
Rape	4,106	5,799	7,800	7,365	10,356	8,198	13,685	27,452	29,929
Robbery	37,967	34,220	36,697	34,308	47,287	57,582	99,461	319,638	351,749
Aggravated assault	36,178	29,803	40,435	50,014	66,226	80,761	137,055	243,817	262,042
Burglary	177,381	194,216	209,190	241,100	329,546	521,799	819,837	1,603,905	1,727,313
Larceny	371,796	516,356	518,115	597,086	821,039	1,294,054	1,907,660	3,233,301	3,319,776
						(971,348)*	(1,362,929)*	(1,940,076)*	(1,972,092)*
Auto theft	121,045	113,704	163,269	104,641	150,356	225,513	390,327	776,100	785,109
Total no. crimes	744,863	900,375	982,183	1,040,249	1,431,066	2,195,150	3,374,112	6,219,879	6,492,926
Total cities	1,423	2,001	2,267	2,069	2,503	3,122	3,798	4,033	4,186
Population	57,222,252	65,128,946	67,608,610	67,465,803	77,450,624	93,599,311	111,798,000	116,634,000	120,090,000

*Over $50

Source: U.S. Federal Bureau of Investigation, *Uniform Crime Reports, 1935-1971* (Washington, D.C.: Government Printing Office).

most comprehensive statistics which exist on national and local crime rates, they are far from an accurate reflection of all crime, much less an indicator of the efficiency of police policy.

While there are approximately 2,800 federal crimes and a great many more actions coded as criminal at the state and local level, these FBI statistics refer only to the seven crimes considered to be the most serious. In this category are four violent crimes against persons (murder, forcible rape, robbery, and aggravated assault) and three crimes against property (burglary, larceny of $50 or more, and auto theft), which are all called "Part I" offenses. Hence, these categories reflect only a small number of the possible criminal acts. They do reflect, however, the criminal acts against persons and property which the public has been conditioned to view as crime.

These statistics are less than totally reliable for a variety of reasons. First, the FBI reports include only those crimes which are considered the most serious, ignoring a great many of the approximately 2,800 federal crimes and numerous other activities which are classified as criminal at the state and local levels. Hence, only relatively detailed information is available concerning those seven crimes which the FBI calls Part I, or serious offenses against person or property.

Further, the exclusive selection of these rather serious and dramatic crimes for inclusion in the crime index of the FBI seems to follow the time-honored tradition of reinforcing the role of the police officer as a crimefighter—doing battle with criminals who are clever inasmuch as they are not concerned with "petty" crimes, and vicious and violent inasmuch as the crimes against persons are sensational and violent.

Third, the production of these crime statistics guarantees neither uniform reporting methods nor comprehensive compilation of *all* Part I crimes. The *Uniform Crime Reports Index* is limited to crimes reported *to* the police and reported *by* the police. There is no crime if citizens do not call the police and the police do not record the crime. In 1965, for example, a study of 10,000 households found that less than one-half of crimes with victims are reported to the police.[3]

There are many reasons for this weakness in police reporting, but three variables are most responsible:

1. The more serious the crime, the more likely it is that it will be reported. Conversely, if the victim sees the crime as not serious then his embarrassment in calling the police for what might appear to be a "silly," or "flip,"

---

[3] Philip Ennis, *Criminal Victimization: A Report of a National Survey* (Chicago: National Opinion Research Center, 1967).

reason may outweigh the outrage or hurt experienced during the victimization.

2. The more likely it is that victim can expect to be reimbursed through insurance, the higher the probability that the citizen will report the crime. Hence, the rate of police notification in the case of auto theft and victimizations as the result of automobile negligence are extremely high.

3. The higher the income of the victim, the more likely the probability that the crime would be reported.[4]

In cases of victims who do not notify the police, the study on criminal victimization conducted by the President's Commission on Law Enforcement and Administration of Justice points to a variety of reasons for such a lack of notification. These reasons fall into four categories:

The first is the belief that the incident was not a police matter either because they did not want the offender to be harmed by the police or because they thought the incident was a private, or at least not a criminal affair. The second is fear of reprisal, either physically from the offender's friends, or economically from cancellation of or increases in rates of insurance. A third set of reasons had to do with the person's not wanting to take the time or trouble to get involved with the police, not knowing if they should call the police, or being too confused to do so. Finally, there is a set of reasons based on attitudes toward police effectiveness. These people believed that the police could not do anything about the incident, would not catch the offenders, or would not want to be bothered.[5]

These occurrences of lack of notification are not the only reasons for the inaccurate levels of crime rate production. The discretionary actions of the police officer, once he is on the scene, influence the production of crime rates. At the scene of a victimization, the police officer must decide whether to fill out a report including an official recognition of the event as a crime, or to ignore the event formally and treat the allegations informally. Further, if the officer decides to treat the victimization as a crime he can influence the production of the crime rate by the type and severity of crime he decides has been committed. If he sees the crime as serious, he adds another notch to nationally publicized statistics; if he sees the crime as minor (Part II Offense), this event will not be part of widely publicized crime statistics.[6]

---

[4] Ibid., pp. 41, 47; and Herbert Jacob, *Urban Justice: Law and Order in American Cities* (New York: Prentice-Hall, 1973), p. 22.

[5] Ennis, *Criminal Victimization*, pp. 43-44.

[6] For a detailed examination of this subject, see Donald J. Black, "Production of Crime Rates," *American Sociological Review*, 34, 4 (August 1970): 733-48.

Hence, it may be that the greatest obstacle to the comprehensive study of crime in America is the shortage of accurate and complete data on the rates and occurrences of criminal victimization. The selective nature of data gathering on the part of the FBI, the deliberately neglectful patterns of police notification by victims, and the differential discretion used by police in choosing how to treat and report an alleged crime all make the process of producing crime rates an almost speculative procedure. However, with these anomalies in mind, it is necessary that we use the Part I Major Crime Index supplied by the FBI because there is no other source of crime data which even approaches this index in completeness and uniformity. These figures have, in the past few years, added to the fear over rising crime and elements of disorder in the nation. Since 1960,

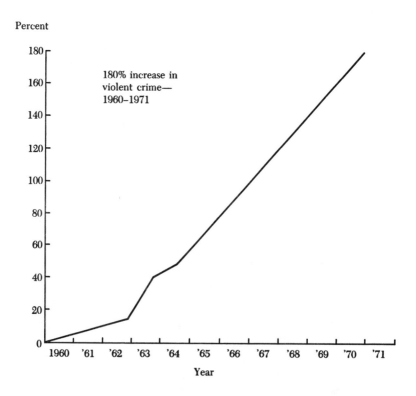

SOURCE: FBI, *Uniform Crime Reports, 1960-1971* (Washington, D.C.: Government Printing Office).

Figure 4

*Crimes of Violence Percent Change Over 1960, 1960–1971
(Includes murder, forcible rape, robbery, aggravated assault)*

they demonstrate a rocketing 180 percent increase in crimes of violence (see fig. 4).

Even more important for the purposes of this volume is the revelation from these statistics that the metropolitan area is the place where the vast majority of not only crimes of violence but also of major crimes against property occurred. As table 4-2 illustrates, in 1971 88 percent of all violent crimes and 86 percent of all crimes against property took place in metropolitan areas which contained 68 percent of the total population. The rural areas of this country had the smallest share of total crimes committed within their regions, and they also had the lowest crime rates per 100,000 of the population.

TABLE 4-2

Violent Crime and Property Crime Rates
(1970–1971)

Area	Violent Crime*	Percent	Property Crime**	Percent
United States				
1970 total	731,402	(100.0)	4,836,795	(100.0)
Rate/100,000	360.0		2,380.5	
1971 total	810,018	(100.0)	5,185,193	(100.0)
Rate/100,000	392.7		2,514.0	
SMSA				
1970 total	641,078	(87.6)	4,121,560	(85.2)
Rate/100,000	457.2		2,939.2	
1971 total	715,731	(88.3)	4,458,185	(86.0)
Rate/100,000	490.6		3,056.1	
Other cities				
1970 total	43,695	(6.0)	401,434	(8.3)
Rate/100,000	181.4		1,666.2	
1971 total	44,522	(5.5)	391,625	(7.6)
Rate/100,000	193.0		1,697.7	
Rural				
1970 total	46,629	(6.4)	313,801	(6.5)
Rate/100,000	120.0		807.4	
1971 total	49,765	(6.1)	355,385	(6.5)
Rate/100,000	133.4		898.9	

*Violent crime is offenses of murder, forcible rape, robbery, and aggravated assault.
**Property crime is offenses of burglary, larceny $50 and over, and auto theft.

Source: FBI, *Uniform Crime Reports, 1970-1971* (Washington, D.C.: Government Printing Office).

Just as the metropolitan area has been the place where most crimes have occurred, it has also been the case that the source of most of this burgeoning metropolitan crime problem has been the big city. Until now, crime in general seems to have remained part of the growing panoply of central city problems while the suburbs have been places to escape the increased crime rates of downtown. However, a recent annual release

of *Uniform Crime Reports* of the FBI provides the first major indications
that this pattern may be reversing itself—at least as far as rate of growth
of crime incidence is concerned. It reports that crime in the United States,
as a whole, decreased by 3 percent during the calendar year 1972 over
1971. While violent crime increased by 1 percent during 1972, property
crimes in general decreased by 3 percent and auto thefts were down by
7 percent. Overall, this 3 percent decrease in crime was the first reduction
since 1955. What is even more significant is that in the large cities of
this nation (200,000 and more) crime was down, on the average, by seven
percentage points. It was only in the central cities of newly emerging
metropolitan areas that cities showed any increase in crime and here the
increase was minimal.

The largest rates of increase in crime were found in the suburbs of
the nation's metropolitan areas. In the large outside central city areas
(less than 50,000 population) and other suburban communities can be found
the most dramatic increases in such crimes as murder (11 percent increase
as opposed to 4 percent increase in cities) and forcible rape (19 percent
increase in the suburbs as opposed to 10 percent increase in the cities)
which heretofore were crimes of only occasional concern to the residents
of the suburbs.[7] It appears that crime, like the metropolitan patterns of
social, economic, and governmental spread and diversity, is also fleeing
to the suburbs.

Collective Violence and the Police

Two other very popular, albeit very stylized, definitions of police in
past decades have been the terms "occupation army" and "pigs." The
former has been used often to characterize the view of police as perceived
by ghetto residents during the urban riots. The latter is a more general
term used by ghettoites and middle- and upper-class white youths to
describe their perceptions of police behavior. The terms have come to
represent a generalized set of perceptions held by distinct and visible
minorities of the metropolitan citizens who view the police as oppressive,
unresponsive, racist, and oftentimes brutal.

A Polemical Approach

Just as it has been argued in chapter 2 that the town and thus the
city became a unit of social control as well as the early settlers' only
contact with policing behavior, so too it has been argued that the city

---

[7] L. Patrick Gray, III, Acting Director, Federal Bureau of Investigation, "Uniform Crime
Reporting," 1972 Preliminary Annual Release (Washington, D.C.: U.S. Department of Justice,
March 8, 1973), p. 1.

is a prime source of social disorder. Many scholars have argued that, since the advent of the industrial city, the city itself is *the source* of disorder. In this spirit, Lewis Mumford has argued that:

> under the aegis of the city, violence . . . became normalized, and spread far beyond the centers where the great collective manhunts and sacrificial orgies were first instituted.[8]

In this tradition, Mumford adheres to the polemics of the privileged and propertied spokesmen of the emerging city. Inherent in this position is the allegation that the city is a destroyer of social ties, primary bonds, and personal efficiency as experienced in agrarian societies.[9] After all, one simply has to look to the major cities of Latin America, Africa, and Asia to see the millions of peasants pushed by abject poverty from the rural hinterlands and pulled to the bright lights of the city. Observers in this tradition have waited for years for the influx of these *classes dangereuses* as they have been termed to force the cities to explode. Finally, while they waited, visible tears in the urban fabric occurred in the 1960s. But the dramatic and well-publicized upsurge of collective violence was not in the Third World, but in the most highly developed of the industrialized powers—the United States.

Perhaps because the United States is the leader of the industrialized world, or perhaps because most observers of collective violence see such violence as aberrant in the United States, but not in the revolution-prone Third World, the American urban riots of the 1960s were not explained from a pure *classes dangereuses* perspective. Rather, scholars of this theory turned to explaining American riots as the product of a few "fearsome strangers"[10] or riff-raff and not a product of the societal concerns of many Americans.

While the word "class" was removed from the label of the explanation of violence, the same perspective was retained. Such disorders were viewed as the result of these few members of a dangerous class of alienated, angry, and crime-prone ghettoites who, because of racial and educational deficiencies, were ill-equipped to live in the social order of the metropolis. Representative of this approach is the report of the Governor's Commission in California after the Watts riot in 1965:

---

[8] Lewis Mumford, *The City as History* (New York: Harcourt, Brace, Jovanovich, 1961), p. 43.

[9] For an assessment of this disciplinary view, see Charles Tilly, "The Chaos of the Living City," in *Violence as Politics: A Series of Original Essays*, ed. Herbert Hirsch and David C. Perry (New York: Harper and Row, 1973), pp. 98-124.

[10] Joe R. Feagin and Harlan Hahn, *Ghetto Revolts: The Politics of Violence in American Cities* (New York: Macmillan, 1973), p. 9.

Many have moved to the city only in the last generation and are totally unprepared to meet the conditions of modern city life. At the core of the cities where they cluster, law and order have only a tenuous hold; the conditions of life itself are often marginal; *idleness* leads to despair and finally, mass violence supplies a momentary relief from this malaise.[11]

Here, as in London and Paris in the eighteenth century, and in New York and Chicago in the nineteenth and early twentieth centuries, the observers of collective violence found an explanation for such events in the unattached and unemployed state of the dangerous classes. In London in 1821, it was reported:

The most superficial observers of the internal and visible apearance of this town, must soon be convinced, that there is a large mass of unproductive population living upon it without occupation or ostensible means of substance; and it is notorious that hundreds and thousands go forth from day-to-day trusting alone to charity or rapine; and differing little from the barbarous hordes which traverse on uncivilized land . . . . The principle of [their] action is the same; their life is predatory; it is equally a war against society, and the object is alike to gratify desire by strategem or force.[12]

In a similar vein in New York, a study of the 1863 Draft Riot concluded that such classes were to be blamed in words very similar to the Watts riot report and the London Report on Police:

There are thousands upon thousands in New York who have no assignable home, and "flit" from attic to attic, and cellar to cellar, . . . still other tens of thousands, poor, hard pressed. . . . Let the law lift its hand from them for a season, or let the civilizing influences of American life fail to reach them, and if the opportunity afforded, we should see an explosion from this class which might leave the city in ashes and blood.[13]

While such an explanation of the New York Draft Riot of 1863 may appear extreme, its dependence upon a dangerous class explanation was no less rhetorical than the Acting Mayor's explanation of the New York Harlem riot of 1964 who blamed the riots first on "so-called fringe groups"

---

[11] Governor's Commission on the Los Angeles Riots, *Violence in the City*, p. 3, as cited in Feagin and Hahn, *Ghetto Revolts*, p. 7. Emphasis added.

[12] George Mainwaring, *Observations on the Present State of the Police of the Metropolis* (London, 1821), pp. 4-5, as cited in Allan Silver, "The Demand for Order in Society," in *The Police: Six Sociological Essays*, ed. David Bordua (New York: John Wiley, 1967), p. 4.

[13] Charles L. Brece, *The Dangerous Classes of New York* (New York, 1872), p. 26, as quoted by Silver, in *The Police*, ed. Bordua, p. 6.

and on "communists and some of the more radical groups," finally saying, "of course a lot of young kids who have nothing better to do get neat fun and delight out of throwing a bottle or a stone at a policeman or anyone else."[14] Later on, the president of the United States, using the FBI reports in the 1964 riots as a source, termed the urban riots the result of the actions of young punks and drunken kids. These new theories of outside agitators, fringe groups, young punks, and other riffraff are all, in part, variants on the time-honored theme of *les classes dangereuses.*

An Alternative View of Collective Violence

From the beginning of the industrial metropolis, the recurrence of collective violence has been common. The contemporary concern and rhetoric over collective violence and crime discussed here draws upon an image of a volatile and naturally unmanageable group of metro-politanites—a "convulsively criminal class at the base of society." [15] While such imagery is part of the class antagonism of the early industrial cities, it is more precisely part of the privileged class fear and distrust of the unemployed, uneducated and culturally alien. Such classes are viewed as the sources of crime and violence. Most forms of civil disturbance or collective violence emanating from such groups either in 1863 or 1973 have been and will, in general, continue to be viewed as aberrant and "as criminal—that is, fundamentally and unconditionally illegitimate." [16]

As if he were speaking of the hopes of contemporary rioters, Silver describes the relationship of elites and rioters of past centuries, pointing out that although the rhetoric of privileged classes of England in the Tory nineteenth century, which deprecated political protest as criminal, demonstrated the very real fears of such elites, this rhetoric should not overshadow the

> evidence for another aspect of this older relationship between elite and agitational population: riots and mobs, however they were feared and defeated, were also means of protest that articulately communicated the desires of the population to a responsive, if not sympathetic, elite.[17]

---

[14] Quoted in the *New York Times*, 22 July 1964, p. 18, as cited in Feagin and Hahn, *Ghetto Revolts*, pp. 7 and 17.

[15] Honorre Antoine Fregier, *Les Classes Dangereuses de la Population dans les Grandes Villes* (Paris, 1840), as quoted by Silver, in *The Police*, ed. Bordua, p. 3.

[16] Silver, in *The Police*, ed. Bordua, p. 15.

[17] Ibid.

In fact Eric Hobsbawn, in his study of pre-industrial city mobs, points to the deliberative nature of the riots—they were, by and large, goal oriented in a collectively subconscious sense. Hobsbawn states that with such riots

> there was the claim to be considered. The classical mob did not merely riot as protest, but because it expected something by its riot. It assumed that the authorities would make some immediate concession: for the "mob" was not simply a casual collection of people united for some *ad hoc* purpose, but in a recognized sense, a permanent entity, even though rarely permanently organized as such.[18]

Just as Hobsbawn, Silver and others have begun to refute, with clarity, the class-biased definition of the early urban riots of the industrial age as the criminal and aberrant reactions of unassimilated members of the dangerous lower classes, so too are contemporary scholars[19] beginning to turn aside the assertions that present-day collective violence is the product of outside agitators, young punks, and other riffraff. On the contrary, Robert Fogelson, in his review of the urban riots of the 1960s, writes that:

> If the survey research, arrest data, and impressionistic amounts are indicative, the rioters were a small but significant minority of the black population, fairly representative of the ghetto resident, and especially of the young adult males, and tacitly supported by at least a large minority of the black community.[20]

He, and others, conclude that the hundreds of riots which touched nearly every black ghetto in the United States between 1964 and 1970 were a

> manifestation of race and racism in the United States, a reflection of the social problems of black ghettos, a protest against the essential conditions of life there, and an indicator of the necessity for fundamental changes in American society.[21]

---

[18] Eric Hobsbawn, *Primitive Rebels: Studies in Archaic Forms of Social Movements* (New York: Norton Paperbacks, 1959), p. 111.

[19] Robert M. Fogelson, *Violence as Protest: A Study of Riots and Ghettos* (Garden City: Doubleday, 1971); Feagin and Hahn, *Ghetto Revolts;* and Alphonso Pinkney, *The American Way of Violence* (New York: Random House, 1972).

[20] Fogelson, ibid., p. 49.

[21] Ibid.

The reflective studies of the urban riots seem to indicate a rejection of the riffraff theory or other popular variations on the dangerous class hypothesis. Instead, there seems to be a significant parallel between the political riots of the sixties and the normative, though pre-political, collective disturbances at the dawn of the industrial city.[22]

Hence the collective violence of the poor is not an occasional or aberrant event in the history of metropolitanism. Just as riots have been a frequent occurrence, so too have observers discovered that the covert and overt collective intents of various mobs or rioters, over time, have been political, aimed at protection and demanding a redress of grievances rather than the sporadic anarchistic outbursts of senseless mobs intent on thrills. Finally, in retrospect we are beginning to discover that the riots of the past decade have served as a violent mirror of the class and race disparities and antagonisms which split the metropolis.

At the vortex of this dichotomy of rhetorical explanations, based on the traditional dangerous class theme versus the revelations that the urban violence of the western industrial age has been more indicative of social demands than of criminal peculiarities, stands the police officer as the agent of social control; the agent-protector of the privileged leaders of the dominant culture; the representative of a racially unrepresentative government and economy (as perceived by those in the ghetto).

As was pointed out in chapter 2, one significant impetus for the creation of police departments was the continuous collective violence which occurred in American cities in the early nineteenth century. From the days of the first formal police departments in New York City and Boston, until today, the continuous spasms of collective violence have forced police departments to affect the role of warriors as they confronted mass demonstrations, mob violence, planned sniper actions, and other forms of guerrilla violence.

Campus Violence

The differences and styles of such contemporary flair-ups are as numerous as the divergent images and experiences of public servants during an occurrence of collective violence. Just as in the case of crime data, from 1964 to the present, there is no way to catalogue with certainty the total number of such violent events in urban areas at any one time. For example, between 1964 and 1970, the most publicized civil disorders seemed to break into two categories: ghetto-based urban riots and campus-based demonstrations. In fact in the latter case, there were 1,792 campus demon-

---

[22] Silver, in *The Police*, ed. Bordua, p. 15.

strations in the 1969-1970 school year alone, accompanied by 14 bombings, 8 deaths, 274 cases of arson, and 7,500 arrests.[23] The recurring explosions on college campuses, which culminated with this last enormous outburst of reaction to the Vietnam War in 1970, brought collective disturbances into the lives of white suburban youths in a way in which the ghetto riots never could. The intrusion of police and national guard during such occasions made the term "pig" one of the most common words in the campus vocabulary and turned many seats of learning into armed and uniformed battle zones.

Ghetto Violence

Although campus disorders have represented dramatic and often horrifying pitched battles between police and citizens, the ghetto riots remain the most graphic statements of contemporary metropolitan collective violence. Even with the visibility and dramatic intensity of the ghetto riots vividly displayed as never before, they still defy precise explanation, definition, and enumeration. The total collective violence reported by any one source for any given period of time will usually differ with another source for a variety of reasons. First, any national total will probably be incomplete—given the limits of access to the sources reporting such events (primarily newspapers, government agencies, and police reports). Further, there is the question of what *is* an act of collective violence or a civil disorder or a riot. These terms are often used interchangeably and yet they seem to suggest different levels and styles of action. Collective violence suggests a more patterned and deliberated style than a riot, which suggests a more spontaneous or unconscious mob action. The term "civil disorder" intuitively suggests less violence than "riot."

Such definitional inferences are clearly evidenced by three different yet major studies of the numbers and severity of urban violence in the 1960s: a study by political scientist Bryan Downes;[24] the Riot Data Review of the Civil Disorder Clearinghouse;[25] and the Report of the National Advisory Commission on Civil Disorders.[26]

Downes subscribes to the term "riot" when discussing violent events. For Downes a riot is a hostile outburst, evidencing specified degrees of

---

[23] "Blueprint for a Super Secret Police," *Newsweek*, 4 June 1973, p. 19.

[24] Bryan T. Downes, "A Critical Reexamination of the Social and Political Characteristics of Riot Cities," *Social Science Quarterly* 51 (September 1970): 349-60.

[25] Lemberg Center for the Study of Violence, Brandeis University "Riot Data Review" (published occasionally in mimeographed form).

[26] *Report of the National Advisory Commission on Civil Disorders* (New York: Bantam, 1968).

arrests, injuries, property damage, and deaths. Between 1964 and the end of 1968, he records 341 such hostile outbursts or "important" riots in 265 cities.[27] He finds that 53,409 persons were arrested for riot-related offenses, 8,459 were injured, and 221 were killed (see table 4-3).

TABLE 4-3

Urban Riots in the United States, 1963–1968

	Riot Data Clearinghouse Compilations*		Downes Compilations**
	Year 1967	April 1968	1963-1968
Number disorders	233 (+ 16E)***	202 (+ 35E)	341
Cities	168 (+ 8E)	172 (+ 34E)	265
Cities with more than 1 disorder (repeats)	39	22	——
States	34 (+ Wash., D.C.)	36 (+ Wash., D.C.)	——
Arrests	18,800	27,000	53,409
Injured	3,400	3,500	8,459
Killed	82	43	221
Property damage	$69,000,000	$58,000,000	——
National Guard			
—Times used	18	22	——
—Numbers used	27,700	34,900	——
Federal troops			
—Times used	1	3	——
—Numbers used	4,800	23,700	——

SOURCES: *Lemberg Center for the Study of Violence, "Riot Data Review."
**Bryan T. Downes, "A Critical Reexamination of the Social and Political Characteristics of Riot Cities," *Social Science Quarterly* 51 (September 1970).
***"E" indicates a riot which was not coded as a *definite* disorder. Such ambiguous cases were coded as "E" or "equivocal" cases by the Lemberg Center.

The Riot Data Clearinghouse conceives of race-related collective violence as "civil disorders." The Clearinghouse uses a more inclusive view of violence and catalogues less important riots than Downes does. Quite specifically, for the Clearinghouse, civil disorder refers to incidents

involving crowd behavior, characterized by either damage to persons or property and/or defiance of civil authority. More specifically, crowd behavior refers to the activities of four people or more acting in concert. Defiance of civil authority is characterized by one or more of the following types of behavior: (1) acts of verbal derision such as chanting, cursing and taunting directed against legitimate local, state and federal officials and such legally-constituted authority; (2) disobedience of the orders of civil authority; and (3) physical attacks upon such authorities and their symbolic equivalents, i.e., police cars, police equipment, police stations, etc.

---

[27] Downes, "A Critical Reexamination . . . of Riot Cities."

Our review of civil disorders is confined to these episodes arising from racial tension. This tension is expressed in episodes of aggressive behavior by blacks against whites or whites against blacks and is characterized by one or more of the following factors: (1) group membership; identification of the participants with their racial group is salient; (2) motivation; individuals become involved in an incident of aggressive behavior because of a sense of injustice or because of their feelings of hostility toward another group. For example, some incidents appear to be set off by events which blacks view as insulting or unjust; others are triggered when an occasion for the expression of hostility presents itself; (3) selectivity of targets of aggression; the targets of aggression, i.e., persons or property, reflect or symbolize the hostility of one group toward another; thus, blacks may attack white-owned property or white persons or policemen as symbols of white authority.[28]

Where Downes recorded 341 important riots between 1963 and 1968, the Clearinghouse, using this definition, recorded 202 civil disorders in the month of April 1968 alone.[29] The violence in this one month occurred in 172 cities in 36 states wherein 27,000 people were arrested, 3,500 people were injured, 43 people were killed, and $58,000,000 worth of property was destroyed (see table 4-2).

While the Riot Data Clearinghouse is credited with one of the most careful accounting processes for the study of collective violence,[30] perhaps the most thorough analysis of the 1967 riots remains the Report of the National Advisory Commission on Civil Disorders. The Commission also found that the definitions of collective violence varied widely. Because of this they found studies which reported as many as 217 civil disorders on the one hand, and as few as 51 on the other, during the first nine months of 1967. Using these sources, the Commission filtered out 164 disorders which occurred in 128 cities and ranked them according to three categories: Major Disorders; Serious Disorders; and Minor Disorders. An incident of urban violence was placed into one of these categories and ranked according to four basic operational indices: degree of violence (fires, looting, sniping); duration of violence (number of days); number of active participants in violent acts; and the level of response the event elicited from police and military sources. After a thorough study of a

---

[28] Lemberg Center for the Study of Violence, Brandeis University "Riot Data Review," no. 1 (May 1968), p. 2. Mimeographed.

[29] It is important to remember that this is the month of the assassination of Martin Luther King. Lemberg Center, "April Aftermath of the King Assassination," "Riot Data Review," no. 2 (August 1968). Mimeographed. This figure does not include 35 "equivocal" incidents in 34 cities.

[30] Feagin and Hahn, *Ghetto Revolts*, p. 102.

sample of twenty-four riot-racked cities, the Commission offered the following generalizations about the ghetto violence of the past few years:

1. No civil disorder was "typical" in all respects. Viewed in a national framework, the disorders of 1967 varied greatly in terms of violence and damage: while a relatively small number were major under our criteria and a somewhat larger number were serious, most of the disorders would have received little or no national attention as "riots" had the nation not been sensitized by the more serious outbreaks.

2. While the civil disorders of 1967 were racial in character, they were not *interracial*. The 1967 disorders, as well as earlier disorders of the recent period, involved action within Negro neighborhoods against symbols of white American society—authority and property—rather than against white persons.

3. Despite extremist rhetoric, there was no attempt to subvert the social order of the United States. Instead, most of those who attacked white authority and property seemed to be demanding fuller participation in the social order and the material benefits enjoyed by the vast majority of American citizens.

4. Disorder did not typically erupt without pre-existing causes, as a result of a single "triggering" or "precipitating" incident. Instead, it developed out of an increasingly disturbed social atmosphere, in which typically a series of tension-heightening incidents over a period of weeks or months became linked in the minds of many in the Negro community with a shared network of underlying grievances.

5. There was, typically, a complex relationship between the series of incidents and the underlying grievances. For example, grievances about allegedly abusive police practices, unemployment and underemployment, housing and other conditions in the ghetto, were often aggravated in the minds of many Negroes by incidents involving the police, or the inaction of municipal authorities on Negro complaints about police action, unemployment, inadequate housing or other conditions. When grievance-related incidents recurred and rising tensions were not satisfactorily resolved, a cumulative process took place in which prior incidents were readily recalled and grievances reinforced. At some point in the mounting tension, a further incident—in itself often routine or even trivial—became the breaking point, and tension spilled into violence.

6. Many grievances in the Negro community result from the discrimination, prejudice and powerlessness which Negroes often experience. They also result from the severely disadvantaged social and economic conditions of many Negroes as compared with those of whites in the same city and, more particularly, in the predominantly white suburbs.

7. Characteristically, the typical rioter was not a hoodlum, habitual criminal, or riffraff; nor was he a recent migrant, a member of an uneducated
underclass, or a person lacking broad social and political concerns.
Instead, he was a teenager or young adult, a lifelong resident of the
city in which he rioted, a high school drop-out—but somewhat better
educated than his Negro neighbor—and almost invariably underem-
ployed or employed in a menial job. He was proud of his race, extremely
hostile to both whites and middle-class Negroes, and, though informed
about politics, highly distrustful of the political system and of political
leaders.

8. Numerous Negro counter-rioters walked the streets urging rioters to "cool
it." The typical counter-rioter resembled in many respects the majority
of Negroes, who neither rioted nor took action against the rioters, that
is, the non-involved. But certain differences are crucial: the counter-rioter
was better educated and had higher income than either the rioter or
the noninvolved.

9. Negotiations between Negroes and white officials occurred during virtually all the disorders surveyed. The negotiations often involved young,
militant Negroes as well as older, established leaders. Despite a setting
of chaos and disorder, negotiations in many cases involved discussion
of underlying grievances as well as the handling of the disorder by control
authorities.

10. The chain we have identified—discrimination, prejudice, disadvantaged
conditions, intense and pervasive grievances, a series of disorder at the
hands of youthful, politically-aware activists—must be understood as
describing the central trend in the disorders, not as an explanation of
all aspects of the riots or of all rioters. Some rioters, for example, may
have shared neither the conditions nor the grievances of their Negro
neighbors; some may have coolly and deliberately exploited the chaos
created by others; some may have been drawn into the melee merely
because they identified with or wished to emulate, others. Nor do we
intend to suggest that the majority of the rioters, who shared the adverse
conditions and grievances, necessarily articulated in their own minds
the connection between that background and their actions.

11. The background of disorder in the riot cities was typically characterized
by severely disadvantaged conditions for Negroes, especially as compared
with those for whites; a local government often unresponsive to these
conditions; federal programs, which had not yet reached a significantly
large proportion of those in need; and the resulting reservoir of pervasive
and deep grievance and frustration in the ghetto.

12. In the immediate aftermath of disorder, the status quo of daily life before
the disorder generally was quickly restored. Yet, despite some notable
public and private efforts, little basic change took place in the conditions

underlying the disorder. In some cases, the result was increased distrust between blacks and whites, diminished interracial communication, and growth of Negro and white extremist groups.[31]

But the "long hot summers" of urban violence are a declining phenomenon. Most political leaders[32] and the most influential organs of the press[33] seem to be convinced, as do most American citizens, that the storm is over. However, Feagin and Hahn, in perhaps the most comprehensive and insightful review of the ghetto riots to date,[33] point out that:

> Caution should also be observed lest we jump to the hasty conclusion that serious ghetto rioting virtually disappeared from the American scene by the year 1970—a conclusion that many leaders and rank-and-file Americans presumably drew from the relatively meager information available to

---

[31] *National Advisory Commission Report*, pp. 110-12.

[32] Feagin and Hahn, *Ghetto Revolts*, pp. 107-8. "One relatively brief analysis of 1967-1971 fact-related civil disorders, recently released by the Civil Disorder Clearinghouse, provides some evidence on the post-1967 trend, although the data are limited just to the three summer months. According to their tabulations the total number of *summer* riots decreased from 176 in 1967 to 46 in 1971. The proportion of the summer revolts that involved what the Clearinghouse termed 'more serious acts of violence,' for example, firebombing and sniping, decreased from 70 percent of the total in 1967 to 53 percent in 1968. Yet the proportion did not decrease significantly between 1968 and 1970; in each of those three summers the proportion of riots encompassing very serious acts of violence hovered around 50 percent. By the summer of 1971 the proportion did decrease again, this time to 27 percent of the total number. However, by other measures of seriousness than those primarily involving the actions of ghetto rioters—such as deaths and injuries among rioters—this stairstep decrease in the level of seriousness over the 1967-1971 period was not confirmed. Although much of the Clearinghouse data supports the conclusion drawn that there was a trend in the direction of a 'cooling" of collective violence between 1967 and 1971, the evidence presented is perhaps more suggestive than conclusive. In particular, one must be careful in generalizing from data on summer riots, since summer riots apparently accounted for less than one-fifth of all race-related civil disorders in the 1968-1971 period." Used by permission of the publisher.

[33] For example, see "What Ever Happened to Black America?" *Newsweek*, 13 February 1972, pp. 29-37. In this issue on "Black America Now," the reporters of *Newsweek* put forth now-familiar descriptions of how black policies in the seventies were received by political leaders and the "establishment" press.
It has been less than ten years since the day a quarter-million petitioners marched on Washington to demand equity for black America. It has been only five since a blue-ribbon Presidential commission warned that, without swift and decisive action, the U.S. would split irretrievably into two societies, black and white, separate and unequal. But now the great surge that carried racial justice briefly to the top of the nation's domestic agenda in the 1960s has been stalemated—by war, economics, the flame-out of the old civil-rights coalition and the rise to power of a New American Majority. Blacks and their special problems have gone out of fashion in government, in politics and in civic concern. "Once again the nation seems weary of the struggle," says Vernon Jordan, the young and temperate executive director of the National Urban League. "There is persuasive evidence that the second Reconstruction is coming to an end." (Copyright Newsweek, Inc. 1972, reprinted by permission.)

them in the mass media. Even the limited research data available indicate that this conclusion is unwarranted, since serious ghetto rioting continued well into the 1970s. Indeed, the Clearinghouse report just discussed notes that there were more instances of race-related collective violence in the "cool" summer of 1971 than in the summer of 1966, considered by many at the time as a "long hot summer." And numerous ghetto riots during the years (not just summers) of 1970 and 1971 attained the level that by National Advisory Commission criteria would be considered "serious" or "major." Thus, even this brief review of the available evidence on ghetto riots during the last decade indicates to us the need for much additional research on the questions of number and seriousness that we have raised here.[34]

The Police and Urban Riots

In one way or another, many of the more proximate reports [35] as well as the more recent reflective studies [36] of the major urban disorders of the 1960s arrive at a conclusion voiced by Robert Fogelson: "The 1960's riots were articulate protests against genuine grievances in the black ghettos." [37] Such an interpretation mirrors that of scholars who have studied similar events of violence in other countries and in this country during other periods.[38] As pointed out earlier by the Riot Commission, the riots symbolized an angry attack on the "symbols of white American society—authority and property—rather than white persons." [39] Such an attack is interpreted not as an anarchistic attempt to disrupt and subvert the order of society but rather as a demand for fuller participation in the authoritative allocation of social goals and more access to the rewards of property. In short, such an interpretation of the ghetto revolts rejects the arguments of those who view such events as the criminal acts of those wild youngsters [40] or riffraff [41] who hedonistically riot for fun and profits [42] and argues instead that the contemporary urban riots stem from grievances which in part arose as a result of

---

[34] Feagin and Hahn, *Ghetto Revolts*, p. 108.

[35] *National Advisory Commission Report;* Nathan Cohen, ed., *The Los Angeles Riots: A Socio-Psychological Study* (New York: Praeger, 1970).

[36] Fogelson, *Violence as Protest;* Pinkney, *American Way of Violence;* Feagin and Hahn, *Ghetto Revolts.*

[37] Ibid., p. 22.

[38] Silver, in *The Police,* ed. Bordua.

[39] *National Advisory Commission Report,* p. 110.

[40] Feagin and Hahn, *Ghetto Revolts,* chapter 1.

[41] Fogelson, *Violence as Protest.*

[42] Edward Banfield, *The Unheavenly City* (Boston: Little, Brown, 1970), pp. 185-209.

the discrimination, prejudice and powerlessness which Negroes often experience. They also result from the severely disadvantaged social and economic condition of many Negroes as compared with those in the same city and, more particularly, in the predominant white suburbs.[43]

As such, the Riot Commission offers the suggestion that the communal diversity of the metropolitan environment with the relative affluence, political power, economic authority, and wealth of property represented by the spreading suburbs when compared to inner-city ghettos compounded the feelings of racial exclusion and economic disadvantage. Such disparitous diversity served as an environment which at least fueled, if not ignited, many of the ghetto outbursts described as urban riots.

The ghetto riots, while they in no way appeared to be organized political protest as were the campus demonstrations, or the nonviolent civil rights marches, still were, by most measured accounts and studies, articulate responses to the diverse and disparate metropolitan environment with all the racial, economic, and political inequities which academics and practitioners have come to ascribe to such social and economic spread and diversity. The role of the police officer in such an environment of systemic inequities and social explosiveness is, at best, tenuous. At this systemic and environmental "macro-level" of discourse, the patrolman stands as the uniformed, white-skinned representative of the dominant political system which is often perceived as deliberately designed, or at least covertly sanctioning, the disparate distribution of authority and property displayed in the findings of the Riot Commission and other studies.

At the day-to-day "micro-level" the tasks the patrolman is paid to perform have often acted as the catalyst precipitating a major civil disorder. In short, the police officer, in his attempt to prevent a breakdown of the social order or a breach of the societal law, often catalyzes such disorder. In attempting to describe the tenuous existence of the police officer in the ghetto, sociologist Jerome Skolnick turned to neither a police officer nor a social scientist but to the eminent black writer James Baldwin. Baldwin cuts to the heart of the oppressive street-level image the police officer presents to the black ghettoite more concisely than the sum of the previously mentioned studies:

The only way to police a ghetto is to be oppressive. None of the police commissioner's men, even with the best will in the world, have any way of understanding the lives led by the people; they swagger about in twos and threes patrolling. Their very presence is an insult, and it would be, even if they spend their entire day feeding gum drops to children. They

---

[43] *National Advisory Commission Report*, p. 111.

represent the force of the white world, and that world's criminal profit and ease, to keep the black man corralled up here, in his place. The badge, the gun in the holster, and the swinging club, make vivid what will happen should his rebellion become overt. . . .

It is hard, on the other hand, to blame the policeman, blank, good-natured, thoughtless, and insuperably innocent, for being such a perfect representative of the people he serves. He, too, believes in good intentions and is astounded and offended when they are not taken for the deed. He has never, himself, done anything for which to be hated—which of us has? And yet he is facing, daily and nightly, the people who would gladly see him dead, and he knows it. There is no way for him not to know it: There are few things under heaven more unnerving than the silent accumulating contempt and hatred of a people. He moves through Harlem, therefore, like an occupying soldier in a bitterly hostile country; which is precisely what, and where he is, and is the reason he walks in twos and threes.[44]

While the specific actions of the police officer may be construed as law enforcement, or order maintenance, or social control, on the street he represents an oppressive army. Whatever the rational measure of his behavior should be, the reaction to an act which might be in Baldwin's terms "insuperably innocent" might be perceived by others as hostile and racially antagonistic.

Before addressing the difficult questions of deliberative malfeasance and brutality on the part of ghetto police, it has already been demonstrated that in the more closely studied riots of the 1960s such environmental conditions attendant to police service have been instrumental in igniting incidents of collective violence. In surveying the riots of 1967, the National Advisory Commission found that police-ghetto encounters were far and away the most likely final precipitous events fomenting urban riots. The more serious the civil disorder, the more likely the probability that the precipitating incident was a local event involving police behavior perceived as unfair or brutal by the people (see table 4-4).

While there has been only limited research on the final precipitous events which ignited the urban riots of the 1960s and while, perhaps, the assassination of Martin Luther King [45] may well be the most dramatic exception to the rule tentatively drawn from the data of the National

---

[44] James Baldwin, *Nobody Knows My Name* (New York: Dell, 1962), pp. 65-67, as cited in Jerome K. Skolnick, "The Police and the Urban Ghetto," in *Race, Crime and Justice,* ed. Charles E. Reasons and Jack L. Kuykendall (Pacific Palisades, Calif.: Goodyear Publishing, 1972), pp. 236-37.

[45] Lemberg Center, "April Aftermath of the King Assassination"; this report points up, as discussed earlier, the importance of the killing of such a revered black man by a white assassin; see also, Feagin and Hahn, *Ghetto Revolts,* pp. 142-48.

TABLE 4-4

Events Which Precipitated Urban Riots: 1967

	All Riots (N=24)	Major Riots (N=6)	Serious Riots (N=10)	Minor Riots (N=8)
Police actions	50%	67%	60%	25%
Negro protest activities	21	33	20	13
Previous disorders in other cities	21	0	10	50
Other	8	0	10	13

SOURCE: Joe Feagin and Harlan Hahn, *Ghetto Revolts: The Politics of Violence in American Cities* (New York: Macmillan, 1973), p. 146. Also the National Advisory Commission on Civil Disorders.

Advisory Commission, police presence as well as police behavior can escalate and even precipitate civil disorder. Inasmuch as the police officer is the uniformed representative of a system which allegedly maintains [46] the disparities and inequities which attend the diverse metropolitan environment, his role in urban riots stands as a dramatic "rorschach" of a part of the dynamics of contemporary metropolitanism.

Police and Corruption

The policeman cannot escape the contradictions imposed upon him by his obligations. He knows that there are many people in the city who think him just a crook in a uniform.[47]

If some metropolitan residents are quick to view the police officer as a member of an occupation army or a pig, others view the police officer as a public servant on the take. Such an image is not necessarily a malevolent one. Few people feel that, when stopped for a traffic violation, they cannot talk the police officer out of a ticket. In fact, a recent study demonstrates that the proper demeanor can often convince the policeman to see things the way the citizen sees them.[48] Most small restaurants in urban areas have special prices for the cop on the beat. Young recruits are told (if they did not know before they joined) that they will be offered free food from the minute they put on their uniform and hit the street.

[46] *National Advisory Commission Report.*

[47] Rubinstein, *City Police*, p. 432.

[48] Black, "Production of Crime Rates."

Rubinstein reports an admonition given by one Police Academy training officer:

> They'll try to buy you with a ham sandwich; don't take it. Put your money on the counter, and if the guy won't take it, leave it for the waitress. You'll see when you go on the beat. Maybe you don't have much money in your pocket, and when you finish your hamburger, the guy says forget it. So you do it once, and then you go down the street and the next guy wants to put a little cheese on the burger for you. Now you're gettin' to like the job.[49]

More than in any country in the world, Christmas in the United States is a time of gift-giving. We give the paper boy "calendar money"; the mailman receives an envelope addressed to *him;* and the police officer receives his bottle (or some other seemingly appropriate Christmas gift such as money or free food). This tradition of Christmas money or the Christmas bottle is found in almost every city in the United States. In the particular case of the police, such practices occur so regularly that it is hard for many to describe them as graft—rarely does money pass hands, and then usually only at Christmas when such money can be considered a gift. However, such practices, so much a part of citizen-police interactions, make it easy for the citizen to start to believe that the police officer can be bought. Every police officer will sooner or later face the temptation of taking a payoff. The most common payoff of money in exchange for a patrolman's acquiescence to the citizen's point of view occurs during traffic offenses. Reporter David Burnham sums up these types of police-citizen interractions:

> Police corruption begins with the notion that policemen by some peculiar divine right are entitled to free meals, free monies, and cut-rate prices on initially everything they buy. This is known as "getting a break." [50]

While Burnham's conclusion points to an acceptance on the part of many policemen that such gratuities are acceptable, it also inferentially leads to common belief on the part of many citizens that the police officer is a corruptible public official. Such forms of graft are so much a part of police behavior that they are quietly accepted by most, if not all, police officers. As such it is unlikely to be ever stopped. Hence, the image of the police officer as corruptible will remain.

---

[49] Rubinstein, *City Police,* p. 401.

[50] David Burnham, "How Corruption is Built into the System—and a Few Ideas for What to Do About It," *New York Magazine,* 21 September 1970.

If these were the only discernible patterns of corruption it would be hardly fair to take too seriously the claim that urban police departments are bastions of corruption and that individual officers are crooks in blue. While such boldly put allegations are still overstatements, there is enough evidence to warrant discussion of such street-level definitions of police. This view of law enforcement could be construed as part of a pervasive cynicism that Americans seem to hold about most institutions and services. A recent Harris Survey paints a picture of this lagging confidence in, or at least ambivalence for, most prominent public and private services (see table 4-5). In this recent six-year period an obvious and dramatic shift has occurred in the public's consideration of its basic institutions. Therefore it would not be totally inconceivable that the cynicism evidenced by a street-level view of the police as corrupt could also be part of the growing lack of confidence leveled against other visible institutions.

TABLE 4-5

Percentage of Persons Having Confidence in
Select Institutions

Institutions of:	Harris Survey	
	1966	1973
The press	29%	18%
Medicine	72	48
Banking and finance	67	39
Science	56	37
Education	61	33
Government:		
Executive	41	27
Congress	42	21
Supreme Court	51	28
Military	——	35
Psychiatry	——	31
Religion	——	30

SOURCE: As cited in a syndicated article by James Kilpatrick, "Confidence in our Institutions" (Washington, D.C.: The Washington Star Syndicate, 1972).

While the view of police as corrupt could be dismissed as part of such universal distrust, there is mounting evidence which suggests other explanations for such a critique of the ethics of police service. This evidence is spotty and far from comprehensively displayed. The very nature of such behavior on the part of law enforcement officials mitigates against an accurate accounting of the actual amount and degree of such activities.

Loosely conceived, more serious occurrences of unethical police behavior can be divided into two areas: political corruption and criminal activities. Political corruption of the police function has been part of the delivery of this service since its inception. The history of the police in urban areas has reflected widespread systematic attempts of political operatives to use the police department as an extension of their machine-like control over the cities.[51] This old-style domination of cities and police departments by political machines employed patrolmen and administrators with the proviso that

> their positions depended upon adherence to the wishes of the political leadership. Many of these men made money for doing illegal things, but basically they were being paid commissions for performing political services, which were a condition of their employment.[52]

Such services included the recruitment and selection of appropriately dedicated personnel; the protection and monitoring of election boxes, and the enforcement of *illegal* licenses to gamble and deal in drugs, liquor, and flesh. Police were even used to serve as bouncers or doormen at speakeasies, after-hours places, and gambling centers.

These latter services, although they were initially tied to political power struggles, especially during the early days of police forces, forced the police into an unholy alliance with political leaders and gangsters.[53] Perhaps the most blatant and flagrant days of police involvement in both political corruption and criminal attitudes were those during Prohibition. During this decade

> every city government sustained in one fashion or another, a beer and liquor trade, and was obliged to protect and then make alliances with professional gangsters and killers. The open collusion between politicians and known criminals outraged even tolerant city people, and the constant revelation that police officials had swollen bank balances angered even "wets" who supported their city governments . . . .[54]

However, with the repeal of Prohibition, the heyday of this triangle of police, politicians, and criminals swiftly diminished. This is not to say that the major administrative positions in diverse cities are still not dependent upon which party is in office. Even more to the point, all the protections of civil service to the contrary, police officers in many systems

---

[51] President's Commission on Law Enforcement and Administration of Justice, *Task Force Report: The Police* (Washington, D.C.: Government Printing Office, 1967), p. 210; Lincoln Steffens, *The Shame of the Cities* (New York: McClure and Phillips, 1904), chapter III; and Rubinstein, *City Police*, pp. 372-75, 3-25.

[52] Rubinstein, ibid., p. 372.

[53] Ibid., p. 372 ff.

[54] Ibid., p. 374.

worry as much about having the proper political affiliation as they do about passing merit exams when they seek promotions. In the course of one study, the case of one officer was observed when he was constantly kidded about taking a merit examination for the position of sergeant. He was told not to worry about passing the exam because it would not help him anyway since he was a Republican and the Chief of Police and City Council were Democratic.[55] In short, politics still plays an important role in most metropolitan police forces. At the county, small city, town and village levels, the amount of political party influence, family tradition, nepotism, and other less formal political factors is even more a part of police service.

The continued influence of political patronage even in the face of civil service reforms is obviously derogatory to the effectiveness of police officers and contributes to the prevalence of corruption within police departments. The President's Task Force Report on Police points out that patronage appointments lower the quality of personnel and encourage all officers to cooperate with politicians. Although a man might withstand this temptation for himself, it may be impossible or even pointless for him to separate himself from the practices of his superior or partners.[56] The result of such patterns of political corruption is a compromise in the delivery of police service from the administrative to the street level.

The other form of police corruption is criminal activity by police officers. Such criminal behavior takes two basic forms: (1) graft and (2) burglary, sale of narcotics, and other *direct* participation in felonious activities. By far the most prevalent of these crimes is graft known also as kickbacks, shakedowns, or payoffs. There is no base information on the percentages of police personnel who participate in graft, but it is relatively commonly accepted that most police agencies evidence some graft at one time or another.[57] The New York City Commission to Investigate Alleged Police Corruption (popularly known as the Knapp Commission) found corruption of the criminal variety to be widespread throughout the New York Police Department. The Commission concluded that it took on a multitude of forms depending upon the criminal activity involved and the level and task of the police officer. Police officers in almost all divisions of the department were found to be on the take while enforcing laws. The Commission found that police corruption appeared to be

---

[55] From unpublished notes, David Perry, "Police Service in a Dual Society: A Study of the Urban Context of Police Service and Its Problems in the City of Rochester, N.Y." Ph.D. dissertation, Syracuse University, 1971.

[56] President's Commission, *Task Force Report,* pp. 210-11.

[57] Rubinstein, *City Police,* p. 375, notes that "no department has entirely eliminated the systematic, regular payoff. . . ."

most sophisticated among plainclothesmen assigned to enforcing gambling laws. In the five plainclothes divisions where our investigations were concentrated we found a strikingly standardized pattern of corruption. Plainclothesmen, participating in what is known in police parlance as a "pad," collected regular biweekly or monthly payments amounting to as much as $3,500 from each of the gambling establishments in the area under their jurisdiction, and divided the take in equal shares. The monthly share per man (called the "nut") ranged from $300 and $400 in midtown Manhattan to $1,500 in Harlem. When supervisors were involved they received a share and a half. A newly assigned plainclothesman was not entitled to his share for about two months, while he was checked out for reliability, but the earnings lost by the delay were made up to him in the form of two months' severance pay when he left the division.

Evidence before us led us to the conclusion that the same pattern existed in the remaining divisions which we did not investigate in depth. This conclusion was confirmed by events occurring before and after the period of our investigation.[58]

Another study reports similar patterns of involvement of police in the protection of criminal behavior in Philadelphia. Here the regular pay-off to the police officer is called a "steady-note" and the study concludes that the elimination of the system of taking a note still

would not resolve the basic problems vice enforcement imposes on police.

The public measures the honesty of its police by the absence of graft and payoffs. The administrators of the police know that . . . even if they control the inclinations of their men to take money, they must continue to struggle to prevent the loosening of standards and the indifference toward lawful conduct that is produced by the constant application of illegal and illicit techniques to make "vice pinches." While many departments have greatly reduced the opportunities for graft which their men may safely take, none has found ways of fulfilling its obligations to regulate public morality without resorting to methods that constantly provide policemen with temptations and encourage ambiguous attitudes toward official standards of conduct. Every police official knows that some of his men are regularly indulging in practices whose legality is questionable at best but cannot be prevented as long as the department demands vice activity. This condition obliges the administrators to rely on ginks, department spies, to ferret out those who step over the line between enforcement and collusion. Every patrolman is guilty of violating some department rule, and whether he is honest or not, every man is on the watch for the ginks.

---

[58] Commission to Investigate Allegations of Police Corruption and the City's Anti-Corruption Procedures, *The Knapp Commission Report on Police Corruption* (New York: George Braziller, 1972), p. 12.

Many of the illegal things that policemen do are not designed to generate payoffs for them but to meet obligations established by the department. If the patrolman were freed from having to make vice arrests, only the corrupt, the money hungry, would continue to do the illegal things so many policemen do.[59]

Hence, for better or worse, the police officer assigned to enforcing vice laws finds himself in a bind. The very nature of the crimes force participation in shoddy, often illegal and/or unconstitutional positions to effect an arrest and, on the other hand, place him in a position which can easily be compromised. In order to get information he is forced to rely on "ginks" or "stooges" and the payment for such information is to turn one's back on the behavior of the ginks. In short, "his information is a form of rent that he collects from local prostitutes, junkies, bums, petty thieves, and burglars." [60]

Direct participation in thefts and burglaries is even more difficult to describe because of the scant information available. However, the President's Commission on Law Enforcement and Administration of Justice reported sporadic patterns in some cities of some officers who

kept stolen property recovered by investigations, stole small items from stores when a patrol inspection disclosed an unlocked door, or emptied the pockets of drunks before they were taken to the station house.[61]

As a case in point they quoted a ranking police official from a southwestern city who described his own participation in thievery and offered his rationale for such behavior:

One night one of our men discovered an unlocked jewelry store. He flushed out the building for a possible burglar, and when he discovered all was secure he checked the safe. It was also unlocked and contained several trays of diamond and ruby rings. He yielded to temptation and took a ring for his wife. He rationalized by thinking the owner would collect insurance when he discovered the loss and that way nobody would really lose.[62]

Similar rationalizations are overtly displayed by some storeowners who, having been burglarized, actually invite the investigating officers to help themselves since "a little more" wouldn't hurt with insurance guaranteeing

---

[59] Rubinstein, *City Police*, pp. 375-76.

[60] Ibid., pp. 382-83.

[61] President's Commission, *Task Force Report*, p. 210.

[62] Ibid.

reimbursement for the loss.[63] Such cynical collusion cannot help but affect some police officers and enhance their cynicism about the real plight of victims of burglaries and, at the same time, make them paranoid about investigating certain crimes. One study describes the cynicism and paranoia that affects the members of one northeastern police force:

> Every patrolman has opportunities to steal. Each time he answers a burglary call or discovers an open property, there is nothing to prevent him from helping himself if his supervisors do not care or are not present. If he is inclined to be a thief, he will be one. There are men who insist on calling their sergeant before entering a private house or require the owner to accompany them if they are present. Many patrolmen do not go in on jobs with some colleagues because they expect to find looting going on; they just drive right past. Some men even risk the ire of colleagues by refusing to handle the paper work for assignments which are theirs if they are not first on the scene.[64]

In conclusion, the street-level conception of the police officer as a crook is not without evidence. It is, however, obvious that the level of political corruption has decreased substantially since the heyday of the old style political machine and Prohibition. Whether there is an increase in collusion between political leaders and the narcotics trade is questionable. At the same time, the level of direct involvement of police officer in graft and other directly criminal acts varies from city to city. Few cities have matched the dramatic patterns of corruption and criminality of New York City; still, most studies concur, no city is *totally* free of at least sporadic acts of criminality. Finally, every city has its share of the traditional if not institutionalized patterns of police-citizen by-play which can strictly pass as corruption.

---

[63] Ibid.

[64] Rubinstein, *City Police*, p. 431.

PART III

Police and the Metropolis

Police and Governments in the Metropolis 5

The crises of the urban environment today suggest the depth and complexity of issues in the management of our society. The city is a thicket of problems, each made more difficult by its interweaving with other nearly intractable problems . . . .

I think we are driven to a significant conclusion: there are some things that are gravely wrong with our society as a problem-solving mechanism. The machinery of the society is not working in a fashion that will permit us to solve any of our problems effectively.

That reality is supremely boring to most social critics. They are extremely reluctant to think about the complex and technical processes by which the society functions. And in the end, their unwillingness to grapple with those processes defeats them.

> John W. Gardiner, The Godkin
> Lectures, Harvard University,
> March 1969.

The crises of the urban environment, including those in education, law enforcement, energy, welfare, employment, health, and the environment, are primarily the functional and fiscal concerns of local governments. As such, the legal and structural responsibility for domestic problem-solving, to use Gardiner's term, resides in local governments in the United States.

As the basic cradle-to-grave services (such as law enforcement) of local governments were augmented by additional services such as public transportation, public welfare, and recreational facilities, the number of local governments increased as well. The disordered tangle of local governments has intensified rather than diminished the problems of the urban environment. Most social critics (as Gardiner points out) are bored by the prospect of analyzing and restructuring these particular aspects of urban problems. Consequently, the tangle of governmental jurisdictions remains an integral part of the structural "thicket" of governmental disorder, and should be included in the consideration of the nature of the police function. This chapter will concern itself with governmental structures and relations, and fiscal patterns.

The category of "governmental structures and relations" can be further broken down into the subcategories of *inter*governmental relations (federal-state-local) and *intra*metropolitan governmental activity. Since local governments not only provide but also partially finance most domestic public services, the fiscal patterns of metropolitan service delivery demand some attention. The structure and politics of financing the metropolis is often broken into distinct categories: the sources of fiscal resources (or revenue) and the allocation of resources among public services (or expenditures). Fiscal characteristics may be used to examine total expenditures and revenues or they may be used selectively to discuss such specific public services as education.[1] The multiplication of local governments and the resulting mismatch of fiscal resources to meet the proliferating demands of metropolitan change have also accompanied discussions of urban poverty, public welfare, and the issues of centralization vs. decentralization.

However, little attention has been paid to the influence of jurisdictional and fiscal patterns on the police function, perhaps because there are relatively few special districts set up exclusively to provide law enforcement compared to the number of special governments set up to provide services such as education, water, sewage services, transportation, and the like. The maintenance of order is rarely established through a "special" government—it is usually part of the general government identified by one's place of residence (village, town, city, or county). In this chapter the police function is discussed in terms of governmental fragmentations and fiscal inequities, and the police function is used to help us understand

---

[1] See, for example, Alan Campbell and Seymour Sacks, *Metropolitan America: Fiscal Patterns and Governmental Systems* (New York: The Free Press, 1967).

the important patterns of governmental spread and diversity. This chapter does not offer a definitive statement of the police in the metropolis from such a vantage point; it is an attempt to support the proposition that such approaches to studying the police function are worthy of further consideration. If the patterns of governmental and fiscal spread and diversity are as important as they appear for metropolitanism in general, and for such selectively studied services as education in particular, then it is quite likely that these patterns are important when analyzing the police function as well.

The Intrametropolitan Growth of Local Governments

While the major purpose of this book is not to discuss in detail the growth and spread of metropolitan governments, the task of this chapter demands at least a short review of the nature of local governance. Such a review necessitates immediate discussion of those features of metropolitan areas which are most common and easily isolated so that some universal features of local government can be used as parameters for our more circumscribed discussion of the governance of the police function. However, the ACIR in its study points out that

> Paradoxically, diversity is the only feature that is common to all metropolitan areas. Few sweeping statements can be made about local government in larger urban concentrations that would not be subject to important qualifications and exceptions. Partly, this is because of the wide range in size and other characteristics of metropolitan areas; partly it is because of the differing historical background of governmental institutions in various parts of the country.[2]

With this warning in mind, we can delineate some features which have been *common* to the process of governmental growth at the local levels and identify some *traditional* types of governmental jurisdictions which seem to be found in most sectors of the nation. Though some of the types of governmental jurisdictions may not be universally a part of metropolitanism in all regions of the nation, they are enough a part of the process of metropolitanism that we can term them common factors of local governance.

---

[2] Advisory Commission on Intergovernmental Relations (ACIR), *Urban America and the Federal System* (Washington, D.C.: Government Printing Office, October 1969), p. 74. This study forms the base for much of the following discussion.

Three common features of local governments are (1) the large number of governments in any one metropolitan area, (2) the smallness of size of local governments, and (3) the overlapping nature of governments, or the layering of jurisdictional responsibilities.

Common Features of
Metropolitan Governments

Metropolitan areas have a large population and a great number of governments. The average metropolitan area in this country has 91 governments, and the average metropolitan county has 48 governments: including 12 municipalities, 7 townships, and 28 special districts (12 of these concerned with the administration of separate school systems), in addition to the general county government. While all this may seem quite startling and confusing, some areas are even more inundated with governments. Metropolitan areas in the Midwest and the Far West, for example, contain more than 100 local governments, and, in some of our largest metropolitan areas, Chicago has 1,113 governments, Philadelphia has 876, Pittsburgh has 704, and New York has 551.[3]

This proliferation in the numbers of governments all but necessitates that the geographic area and the number of residents found in most of these governments will be relatively small. Given that approximately three-quarters of all metropolitan residents reside in such jurisdictions, let us look at the size of municipalities in SMSAs. Even with the overriding residential popularity of municipalities,

> about half of the nearly 5,000 municipalities in the SMSAs have less than a single square mile of land area, and only one in five is as large as four square miles. Two-thirds of them have fewer than 5,000 residents and one-third fewer than 1,000.[4]

Small size and multiple governments result in fragmentation of service delivery in metropolitan areas. A layering of governments or overlapping of jurisdictions is a third common feature of government in metropolitan areas. The average metropolitan resident is serviced by no less than four separate governments, examples of which are a county, a municipality, a school district, and one of several types of special districts. The ACIR study points out that

> the average central city has more than four overlying local governments, and in parts of some metropolitan areas the number of layers is much greater.

---

[3] Ibid., pp. 75 and 117.
[4] Ibid.

As a rule, the boundaries of various local government units are not coter-minous: less than one-fifth of the school districts and only one-eighth of the special districts in SMSAs coincide geographically with a municipality, township, or county.[5]

Traditional
Jurisdictions

Certain basic types of local government are found in the metropolis. As described in chapter 2, from the earliest days of the Republic there have been two basic classes of government: the county and the munici-pality. Counties were created to serve both a general and a distinct purpose. First, they were established as the administrative arm of the state govern-ment at the local level, handling such state functions as conducting elec-tions, recording documents, maintaining courts, and administering state law. Second, they were established to provide services to the rural unincor-porated regions. Such services included keeping the peace and building and maintaining farm-to-market roads. Counties exist as important units in all states except New England, where the town still remains the essential state as well as municipal unit. In other states, the town soon gave way to the incorporated municipality—called either a city, village, or a town.

Municipal units of government came into existence as residential centers and grew to urban stature, demanding additional service which the county or the state could not directly provide. As a result, the states through a variety of general laws authorized such residential sectors requiring urban-type service to raise revenues through taxes and bonds, and with these revenues to provide a specified range of local services to the citizenry. The larger the incorporated municipality, the greater the range of services it is authorized to provide. The core municipality (or central city) is often considered a general service provision district when compared to the single-purpose special districts which have become so common in areas outside large municipalities.

The first of the special districts was created in the early nineteenth century due to the development of public education. The first distinct single-purpose special district was the school district. As we indicated earlier, the school district is much smaller than the county and often much smaller than the municipality—for example, the city of San Antonio, a large general service provision municipality, also has five school districts. Of the 20,745 local governments in metropolitan areas, approximately one-quarter or 5,018 are school districts. Another 7,049 special districts represent the proliferation of primarily single-purpose governments created

---

[5] Ibid.

to meet the crises brought on by the increased crush of metropolitan growth (see table 5-1).

The creation of these special districts is a memorial to the disorder of local institutions attempting to meet one crisis after another—first establishing a new fire district and then a new water district and then perhaps public housing. These districts are usually found outside the central cities of the metropolitan area and are created by municipalities with only limited general service provision responsibilities or by townships or boroughs that are unincorporated. In short, they represent the attempt of suburbs to paste together a governmental pattern which is not as comprehensive in its service provision as the cities they surround. Such attempts have resulted in a 15 percent increase in special districts since 1962 in SMSAs. Nationally, the number of special districts has almost doubled in the past twenty years, with most of this increase occurring inside metropolitan areas. One of the most compelling reasons for the increase of special districts is the set of limitations placed on already existing governments to create more revenue. Coupled with this fiscal limitation is the inability of the rurally focused county government to provide for the burgeoning numbers of suburb-bound residents and the urban-type services they demand.

TABLE 5-1

Local Governments within SMSAs by Type—1962, 1967

	1962°		1967
All governments	21,817	(18,442)	20,703
School districts	7,072	(7,606)	5,018
Other	14,745	(12,438)	15,685
Counties	407	(310)	404
Municipalities	4,903	(4,142)	4,977
Townships	3,282	(2,575)	3,255
Special districts	6,153	(5,911)	7,049

°As defined in 1967.

SOURCE: U.S. Bureau of Commerce of Government, 1967, Vol. I, *Government Organizations* (Washington, D.C.: Government Printing Office, 1968), p. 29.

A final style of governance at the local level exists in the unincorporated area of the county. A study of such areas points out that:

First of all, many such areas are large in population and territory; in fact, although generally less densely settled, a considerable number of them contain more land than the cities they border. Second, virtually all unincor-

porated urban areas are wholly or predominantly residential, usually medium-
or low-income developments, rather than commercial or industrial, and
consequently tend to have limited financial resources. Third, their residents
frequently resist annexation or incorporation, preferring to choose services
cafeteria-style—that is, to select a few public services that meet, sometimes
only in part, their most pressing needs from whatever sources are willing
to provide them, whether a private company, one or more special districts,
the county, or even the adjoining city. Fourth, many urban fringes are
seriously deficient in some or even all basic urban-type services and regulatory activities; water supply, garbage collection, streets, sewerage, fire protection, police protection, parks and recreational facilities, zoning controls,
and subdivision regulations.[6]

The Metropolis and the
Federal System:
Intergovernmental Relations

Although interpretation of the law places the vast majority of the
responsibility for the provision of domestic services with the local governments, it should be underscored that the local governments just discussed
are all the legal creations of the states. As such, the state has ultimate
responsibility for structurally defining the shape of the service jurisdictions
and the amount of responsibility for a service which will rest with the
locality. The ACIR points to the role of states in creating the situation
of fragmented chaos:

> As the road to the present urban hell was paved, many major sins of
> omission and commission can be ascribed to the States. Cities and suburbs,
> counties, townships, and boroughs alike are, after all, legal creations of the
> State. The deadly combination of restricted annexation and unrestricted
> incorporation; the chaotic and uncontrolled mushrooming of special districts;
> the limitations upon municipal taxing and borrowing powers; the deliverance
> of the all-important police powers of zoning, land use and building regulation
> into the hands of thousands of separate and competing local govern-
> ments—these are but a few of the byproducts of decades of State government
> nonfeasance and malfeasance concerning urban affairs.[7]

Further, since 1920 there has been a significant increase in the role
of the federal government in domestic affairs. During the Depression days

[6] John C. Bollens and Henry J. Schmandt, *The Metropolis: Its People, Politics and Economic
Life* (New York: Harper and Row, 1965), pp. 419, 420. Used by permission of the publisher.
See also John C. Bollens, "Urban Fringe Areas—A Persistent Problem," *Public Management*
42 (October 1960): 218-21.

[7] ACIR, *Urban America and the Federal System*, p. 2.

of the 1930s, the federal government enacted a few grant-in-aid programs aimed at alleviating some of the hardships of the economic chaos of the era. There were more than 400 grant programs to local areas by the 1960s, most of which found their way into metropolitan regions of the nation. To offset the confusion of governments at the local level and the neglect of public issues at the state level, the federal government initiated a phalanx of programs and grants along categoric lines—detailing the purpose for the funds and setting in motion an institutional arrangement

> characterized by a chain of direct Federal-State-local functional and professional communication—bypassing in many instances the decision making prerogatives of Cabinet officers, the Executive Office of the President, Governors, legislators and county commissioners.[8]

With each new grant program came a new entourage of specialists and subspecialists at all levels of government. Such professionals created enough of a closed system through such programs that "few, if any, counter balancing efforts were made to strengthen the position of the department secretaries, the Governors, or the mayors." [9] In short, by the end of the late 1960s, the federal government had come to provide, through billions of dollars in categorical grants and other monies, substantial governing influence in metropolitan areas. In response, the federal government has quickly begun to move away from the "empire building" nature of the categorical grants of the past toward a revenue sharing and block grant philosophy. Whether or not the beneficial aspects of allocating federal funds without concomitant federal direction to the disorganized local governments or the lethargic state governments will outweigh the evils of empire building remains to be seen. In any case, the role of both the federal government and the states in the provision of public services at the local level cannot be ignored.

The Spread and Diversity of Police Districts

From the earliest days of the Anglo-Saxon tradition, the repression of crime has been considered a prime responsibility of governments. In line with this tradition in the Western world, since the earliest organization of towns in the United States the local government has been the most

---

[8] Ibid.

[9] Ibid., p. 3.

active level of responsibility for policing and law enforcement. In fact, as discussed in chapter 2, one of the main purposes for the development of the organization of the New England town was to protect people and property in the early settlements. The town was the only experience that the early settlers had with law enforcement in the colonies.

Consequently, the police function in this country has been primarily a function of the incorporated local governments, counties, and the states. With few exceptions, as we will discuss later, police service has not been provided by special districts. Given its close association with the general purpose of government to provide social order, most local governments have taken upon themselves some semblance of order maintenance and law enforcement through a police department.[10]

Increases in the number and distribution of governments performing the police function at the local level have, therefore, accompanied the rapid growth of the disorganized and fragmented urban "thicket." In fact, when the structure of police districts in the United States is compared against the order and growth of the police function in other parts of the world (such as England and France where the police function is centrally provided at the national level), some scholars find no other explanation than "historical accident." [11] No other nation in the developed world has such a disorganized and unstructured organization of governance when it comes to police. It seems that the propensity for decentralized government services at the metropolitan level and the strong tradition of local control over the law enforcement function have coalesced to guarantee that the provision of police service stands as a perfect example of the governmental spread and diversity which, in part, embodies what we have termed "metropolitanism." As one scholar puts it:

> Regardless of size, location in relation to other units of general local government, or financial resources, each unit of government is deeded "capable" of administering basic law enforcement within the confines of its own jurisdiction.[12]

Such a firm retention of local responsibility for enforcing the laws has resulted in highly decentralized and fragmented control of the police function. This local condition coupled with the responsibilities undertaken

---

[10] I emphasize *most* traditional forms of government here because some unincorporated governments and a minority of incorporated governments do not have police departments.

[11] George E. Misner, "Recent Development in Metropolitan Law Enforcement," *Journal of Criminal Law, Criminology and Police Science* 50, 5 (January-February 1960): 499-508.

[12] Ibid., p. 497.

by the state and federal governments has created a fragmented police structure which is also overlapping.

In any given metropolitan area in the United States, it is possible to find police officers from federal, state, county, and municipal agencies, as well as auxiliary, honorary, reserve, and private agents. In some areas there are also police agents attached to special districts such as harbors or parks. It is practically impossible to arrive at an accurate total of police units and officers in the nation as a whole, much less supply a definitive figure of those agencies and officers found only in metropolitan areas. The vast array of police agencies and definitions of official responsibility all but preclude anything but a rough estimate.

The number of police districts serving the nation as a whole is staggering (see table 5-2). There are approximately 40,000 local agencies of law enforcement, over 3,000 county departments, 200 state agencies, and 50 different agencies at the federal level which can, for one reason or another, undertake police activities at the local level. The overall number of agencies within metropolitan areas has increased with the growth in the number of metropolitan areas, as well as in the number of municipalities within metropolitan areas. In 1960 it was reported that there were more than 3,600 units of local government involved in the police function in one way or another. This amounted to more than twenty police agencies per metropolitan area on the average.[13] However, when the last comprehensive

TABLE 5-2

Law Enforcement Agencies in the United States

Number of Personnel	Level	Number of Agencies
	Governmental (Paid)	
25,000	Federal	50
30,000	State	200
35,000	County	3,050
200,000	Municipal	3,700
35,000	Townships, Towns Boroughs, Villages	33,000
	Governmental (Non-Paid)	Operated by
425,000	Auxiliary, Honorary, Reserve, Voluntary	Governmental Agencies
	Private	
250,000	Guards, Investigators, Watchmen, Doorkeepers	5,000
1,000,000 people	Totals	45,000 units

SOURCE: A.C. Germann, Frank D. Day, and Robert R. J. Gallati, *Introduction to Law Enforcement* (Springfield, Ill.: Charles C. Thomas, 1966), p. 153.

---

[13] Ibid., p. 500.

study was done, there were at least 243 SMSAs and more municipalities which logically added to the numbers of metropolitan police agencies. Germann, Day, and Gallati, in reviewing this phenomenon in light of what it tells us about local control of the police function, state:

> Yet, when one studies the metropolitan areas of the United States from a police standpoint, and observes the urban, the suburban, and the rural areas involved, often several counties, municipalities, townships, and villages are found, and, as well, from fifty to one hundred police agencies.
>
> Thus, local control, as it relates to the metropolitan areas, results in many chiefs of police, police commissioners, city managers, councilmen, and consequently, many differing policies relating to police operations.[14]

Whether we use an average or a more precise figure of police "governments," the stark fact remains that these agencies add to the overall magnitude of the proliferation and fragmentation of services in an already fragmented and disorganized metropolis.

The metropolitan area of Detroit graphically displays the condition of overlap and fragmentation of police government. As figure 6 illustrates, Detroit is plagued by a large number of police units spread about the metropolitan region. Almost 78 percent of the 85 police units servicing the area have less than 50 members, and 30 percent have less than 20 members. The Detroit Police Department alone, which has 4,682 members, has more members than the combined personnel of the other 84 departments.

The size of the Detroit police force should not be construed as inordinately large, especially when compared to Los Angeles, which has 5,018 officials, and New York City, which has approximately 37,500 police employees. On the other hand, some cities within metropolitan areas have police departments composed of only one employee. The overall inconsistency of such a ritualistic adherence to local control of the law enforcement function is rather dramatic testimony to the fact that the basic structure of law enforcement has not really changed since the turn of the century. What has changed is the nature and diversity of population centers and the law enforcement demands which such diverse centers of living place upon the local structures.

There is no way to compare the competencies of large central city police forces and single-man suburban police units. They often have similar duties, but not comparable resources. While the local police departments are generally responsible for administration of all law in their respective

---

[14] A. C. Germann, Frank D. Day, and Robert R. J. Gallati, *Introduction to Law Enforcement* (Springfield, Ill.: Charles C. Thomas, 1966), p. 135.

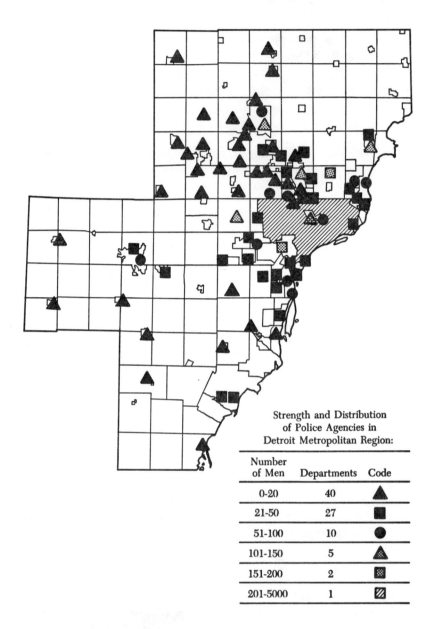

Strength and Distribution
of Police Agencies in
Detroit Metropolitan Region:

Number of Men	Departments	Code
0-20	40	▲
21-50	27	■
51-100	10	●
101-150	5	▲
151-200	2	▨
201-5000	1	▨

SOURCE: The President's Commission on Law Enforcement and Administration of Justice, *Task Force Report: The Police* (Washington, D.C.: Government Printing Office, 1967), p. 69.

Figure 5
Fragmentation of Urban Police in the Detroit SMSA

districts, a review of the types of police units attached to the traditional jurisdictions of local government found in metropolitan areas provides a pattern of overlapping and fragmented duties. The next three sections will discuss (1) the nature of the police function as found in different jurisdictions of governments in the metropolis, (2) the content of the police function carried out by state and federal governments within the metropolitan areas, and (3) the general features of service delivery at the local level which characterize the police.

Policing the Traditional Jurisdictions of Local Government

Police Departments in Cities

The municipality designated as a "city" is the most discussed form of incorporated government found in the metropolitan area. The most visible of the metropolitan cities are the central cities, the jurisdictions possessing the greatest share of the nation's urban problems. On the other hand, the small cities outnumber the central cities in the metropolis. These small municipalities have sprung up around many of the central cities. One of the main reasons is to set up incorporated bunkers in an attempt to avoid being annexed the central cities. Hence the city is a jurisdiction which includes communities of all sizes and provides a ratio of police personnel to citizenry which ranges all the way from 0.1 police per 1,000 population to 9.3 police per 1,000 population.

In such communities, whether there are two or 5,000 police officials, the agency is responsible for crime prevention techniques such as educating the public to the patterns of crime, cooperation with parole personnel, and the like. They must also engage in crime detection and repression activities which include investigating crime, apprehending suspects, recovering stolen property, and assisting the courts in prosecuting alleged offenders. Further, whether an agency is large or small it must participate in non-crime related activities such as controlling the orderly flow of traffic in the community, crowd control, and police community relations.

All city police agencies, regardless of their staff resources, are required to provide general information services, emergency assistance, and special services such as licensing and registration. Finally, there is a common responsibility for all city police units to guarantee the personal liberties of the citizens from unlawful intrusion by the government. Such services are carried out by the multitude of municipalities in the metropolis as each acts to retain its control over the administration of the police function.

The County Sheriff's Department

Although the structure of city police departmental jurisdictions displays the influence of the tradition of local control over the police function, the office of the county sheriff is perhaps an even more dramatic throwback to the earliest development of the constabulary. During an analysis of the contemporary sheriff's office, one text presents a description that is not at all dissimilar to earlier assessments of colonial police departments:

> The duties of the County Sheriff vary with the county. He may be sheriff, coroner, assessor, tax collector, public administrator, overseer of highways and bridges, custodian of the county treasury, keeper of the county jail, court attendant, executor of criminal and civil process, major law enforcement officer, or executioner.
>
> In most counties, he must be twenty-one years of age, a citizen, and a registered voter or on the tax rolls. No physical, educational, or moral qualifications are demanded. No knowledge of law or of law enforcement is necessary.[15]

For the most part, the county sheriff is an elected official who can take office with no law enforcement training. Hence he serves for two, three, or four-year terms with more attention paid to his political competence than to his professional ability. Not only are the administrative and professional abilities of the county sheriff ignored in the elective procedure, but also in many counties, both within and outside of metropolitan areas, the income of the county sheriff is dependent upon fees he receives from serving the courts, managing jails, serving writs, arresting federal offenders (such as persons AWOL from the Armed Forces) and the like. He is also able to gain personal remuneration for his duties by retaining the difference between the amount of money he spends while carrying out certain responsibilities (such as serving food to prisoners) and the amount of money provided him by the county government. In the tradition of the old constabulary, the sheriff has the right to deputize anyone he feels can be helpful in an auxiliary, reserve, or honorary capacity. In short, a county sheriff's office is often not run in terms of modern police professional tactics.

The primary jurisdictions within SMSAs to which the sheriff's office is responsible are those unincorporated areas within metropolitan areas. Second, some sheriff's offices also maintain contractual agreements with some municipalities who find their own police department too small, or who prefer not to maintain an agency of law enforcement administration.

---

[15] Germann, Day, and Gallati, *Introduction to Law Enforcement*, p. 126.

At times, the county sheriff's office works in conjunction with other police agencies in the metropolitan area through informal agreements, formal arrangements (agreements), or partnerships in regional service programs.

From this brief review of the county sheriff's office, it should be apparent that few police units at the local level are as dependent as the sheriff's department upon the personal style of their chief official. The county office is often run in an "informal" and political manner. In conclusion, the county sheriff's office represents the inconsistency of local government and its rigid resistance to change.

Police in the Towns, Boroughs, and Villages

These smaller communities which comprise sections of the incorporated area surrounding the central city possess nearly every style of police unit imaginable. The smallest and most rural of these communities, still relatively untouched by the social and economic spread and diversity of metropolitan growth, usually have part-time, short-term, nonprofessional police. These police, like the county sheriff, are often elected and are paid on a fee basis. This system of law enforcement has been jealously maintained, even by those communities which have begun to experience metropolitan growth. Such communities are often attempting to retain their small-town flavor and the tradition of local autonomy. The adherence to small town constabulary systems is sometimes a result of distrust and fear of the types of police systems practiced by their neighbors, especially the advanced systems of policing found in the big central cities.[16]

However, the struggle with metropolitan growth for most small townships, villages and boroughs often ends with full-time salaried police personnel who, in a limited way, attempt to mirror the more professional practices of the larger sister cities. Many towns have begun to establish advanced programs of crime detection and prevention and traffic control.

Special District Police Forces

The least common form of jurisdictional arrangement of the police function is the special district. However, many metropolitan areas do possess one or another special police units such as park police, harbor patrols, turnpike police, and bridge patrols. More recently, various police functions have been consolidated into metropolitan, county, or region-wide service districts which, while they do not compose a differently uniformed and organized police force, do consolidate a number of police departments

---

[16] Ibid., p. 132.

under a single operation in order to provide a specific service over a broader area than any one of the member police forces covers alone. Functions such as communications, training, record keeping, and crime lab facilities are examples of special jurisdictional realignment.

Conclusion

A cursory glance at the patterns of intrametropolitan police forces finds very little order in the vast array of police institutions. Each local government, if it prefers, has the right, through long-standing tradition, to keep the police function and to select, train, and pay police officers in any manner which it deems reasonable. Hence, where the larger central city usually has large numbers of professionally trained officers working for designated salaries and with equipment and structures which are relatively advanced, the smallest communities and counties often practice the police function in a very different manner. The rights of local autonomy fragment uniform police practices and often jurisdictional overlap compounds the confusion caused by such fragmentation. As such, the provision of police service within metropolitan areas by local governments is highly decentralized. This decentralization is clear and dramatic evidence of the disparate problems facing contemporary law enforcement and also stands as an example of governmental spread and diversity in the metropolis.

State Participation in the Police Function

State agencies further complicate the pattern of governmental overlap. For the nation as a whole, there are no less than 200 state agencies which, in one way or another, provide some portion of the police function at the local level. Obviously some states have many more such agencies and compose much more of this total number of law enforcement units than do other states. Further, some of these units possess general police power, others perform some special task and still others are simply regulatory agencies.[17]

There is no baseline from which to argue that, at some fundamental level of police activity, the state agencies of law enforcement administration provide all portions of the state with comprehensive and uniform service. On the contrary,

---

[17] See ibid. for a detailed discussion of the state and federal agencies involved in the police function. In particular, see pp. 139-55.

barely half (of the state police forces) have statewide investigative authority; only seven carry a full range of police responsibility. Everywhere, they are thinly spread and mainly oriented towards highway patrol. This preoccupation leaves most of them without the means—even where they have legal authority—to provide investigative or other support for weak local forces.[18]

When the average citizen thinks of law enforcement administration at the state level, he invariably thinks of the state police. There are two basic types of state police: those empowered to enforce all the laws of the state, and those specifically designated as highway patrols. The former type of state agency acts as a police department with the responsibility for all phases of police work, including crime detection, traffic, control, record collection, organized crime, and so on. The latter type of state agency, which is more common, is primarily responsible for protection of the motorist and the regulation and licensing of private and commercial vehicles.

At a more particular level, the remainder of the law enforcement agencies of the states covers a variety of special functions. In one state or another various types of police agencies can be found, including identification or record keeping units; statewide, centrally located, crime labs; liquor control boards; public health agencies; special-purpose investigative units (such as narcotics, organized crime); and practically every other type of civil or criminal investigation unit. Various state departments such as finance, agriculture, commerce, insurance, mental health, civil service, labor-industrial relations and the like often have additional investigative and enforcement agencies concerned with civil and criminal misbehaviors.

In short, there is every indication that much of the fragmentation and disorganization found at the local level is also visible at the state level. There are few states where a great deal of commonality or agreement can be found concerning the structural and institutional designation of the police function. Rather than providing regional control, direction, and support for those local police forces which suffer the most from their limited jurisdictional scale and weak personnel, execution of police administration by most state units appears to add to the confusion. While some states have moved to resolve some of the disparities created by the contemporary structuring of the police system, none have attempted to confront the barriers of local autonomy and the resulting service problems with anything that begins to approximate a comprehensive program of expansion and strengthening of state agencies to address local needs, especially in

---

[18] CED, *Reducing Crime and Assuring Justice* (New York: Council for Economic Development, 1972), p. 31.

areas without effective law enforcement agencies.[19] It seems to be almost universally accepted that one of the most important reforms in American law enforcement should be the expansion, strengthening, and comprehensive modernization of the police function at the state level.[20] Here, as in other public service areas, the state appears to be a reluctant or at least confused partner in intergovernmental relations.[21]

The Federal Role in the Police Function

We began this discussion with the premise that law enforcement has traditionally been given the rights of "local automony" and is primarily a local function. However, just as the states obviously carry out a broad range of police functions, so does the federal government involve itself in providing financial and technical assistance as well as direct anti-crime service to local jurisdictions. Up to fifty federal agencies are concerned with law enforcement functions in at least a tangential manner and at least fifteen federal agencies are directly involved in the administration of programs designed to reduce crime at the local level. The major categories for such programs include:

1. support and improvement of federal, state, and local law enforcement agencies,
2. reform and enforcement of federal criminal laws,
3. court administration and prosecution,
4. custody and rehabilitation of offenders,
5. prevention of crime,
6. planning and coordination of state and local crime activities, and
7. crime and research statistics.[22]

Those federal agencies which actually deploy personnel or carry out programs at the local level concerning the enforcement of particular laws are those directly involved in the police function, and they include the

---

[19] Ibid.

[20] See the President's Commission on Law Enforcement and Administration of Justice, *Task Force Report: The Police* (Washington, D.C.: Government Printing Office, 1967); ACIR, *Making the Safe Streets Act Work: An Intergovernmental Challenge* (Washington, D.C.: Government Printing Office, 1971); CED, *Reducing Crime and Insuring Justice;* and Germann, Day and Gallati, *Introduction to Law Enforcement.*

[21] Roscoe C. Martin, *The Cities in the Federal System* (New York: Atherton Press, 1965), pp. 45-82.

[22] ACIR, *Making the Safe Streets Act Work,* p. 1.

Department of Justice; the Treasury Department; the Post Office Department; the Department of Transportation; the Department of Labor; the Department of the Interior; and the Department of Agriculture. As table 5-3 indicates, the scope of federal police activity is quite broad, and the rather particular responsibilities of federal agents at the local level further demonstrates the overlapping and fragmented nature of public policy execution in the contemporary metropolis.

TABLE 5-3

Federal Agencies Deploying Personnel at the Local Level°

Executive Dept.	Agency Personnel	Police Function
Dept. of Justice	Criminal Div: FBI; Fed. Prosecutors; U.S. Marshals and other law enforcement personnel such as Bureau of Narcotics and Dangerous Drugs	Detect; identify and apprehend violators of federal laws
Treasury Dept.	Bureau of Customs; Secret Service; Internal Revenue Service	Customs violation; forgery; protect chief executive; alcohol; tobacco laws
Post Office Dept.	Postal Inspectors and other personnel	Mail fraud and theft; monitor of illegal materials transfers
Dept. of Interior	U.S. Park Police	Fed. game laws; supervise Indian reservations; park laws
Dept. of Transportation	U.S. Coast Guard; Federal Aviation Admin. police	Criminal laws in U.S. waters; water pollution laws; aircraft hijacking
Dept. of Labor	Agencies interested in regulation of unions	Illegal use of union pension funds
Dept. of Agriculture	Consumer Protection related bureaus	Consumer fraud

°This listing is not an exhaustive compilation—the intent of this table is to demonstrate the broad range of federal officials performing police activities at the local level.
SOURCE: Advisory Commission on Intergovernmental Relations, *Making the Safe Streets Act Work: An Intergovernmental Challenge* (Washington, D.C.: Government Printing Office, 1971).

Perhaps the greatest amount of federal activity in the fight against crime comes in the form of programs which the federal government supports through direct legislative action and funding or at least through supportive grants. A variety of executive agencies, nine executive departments, and the judicial branch of the government provide substantial amounts of money and program support for the reduction of crime at the local level (see table 5-4).

As table 5-5 demonstrates, the amount of the federal government's fiscal participation in almost every phase of the police function is increasing steadily, although major contributions are a recent phenomenon. The role of the federal government as a fiscal supporter of local efforts is probably even more impressive than the direct federal agencies of law enforcement. While the amount of money the federal government spent between 1969 and 1971 on direct agency activities involved in "federal criminal law enforcement" rose from slightly more than $365 million to approximately $472 million, its overall importance as part of the federal law enforcement effort as measured by percentage of total program dropped from 54 percent of the total federal outlay to 38 percent. At the same time, such activities as law enforcement support and planning and coordination of crime reduction programs jumped from 8 percent to 19 percent and from 2 percent to 18 percent, respectively. Such supportive and directive programs are now about as much a part of the federal crime effort as direct federal personnel deployment (see table 5-6).

The Results of Governmental Spread and Diversity

The more particular results of decentralization of administrative units can be broken into at least four general areas: conflicts in policy arising from differences in personality and power; variations in administrative procedures; diverse interpretation of laws; and jurisdictional confusion.

Policy Differences Arising from Political and Personality Conflicts

Police departments are no different than any other agency when it comes to disagreeing about service delivered. Each police district represents a distinct province of police authority with differing power and policy apparatuses. The chief executive of such units is elected by the citizenry of the jurisdiction or appointed by the legislative arm or the chief administrator of the local government. These differing patterns of designation of the chief police executive result in different patterns of administrative responsibility; the police chief is responsible to the chief

TABLE 5-4

Federal Outlays for the Reduction of Crime
(in thousands of dollars)

Agency	1969 Actual		1970 Estimate		1971 Estimate	
	Direct	Support	Direct	Support	Direct	Support
Department of Justice	329,136	61,179	387,078	211,864	427,134	403,294
Treasury Department	90,344	0	125,578	0	141,903	0
Department of Health, Education, and Welfare	22,848	22,585	25,463	34,704	27,673	48,092
The Judiciary	48,485	0	55,510	0	58,054	0
Post Office Department	31,899	0	27,904	0	36,509	0
Department of Housing and Urban Development	0	526	0	13,360	0	23,600
Veterans Administration	3,700	6,963	4,100	11,357	7,000	15,501
Department of Interior	14,523	1,000	16,813	1,752	17,931	1,782
General Services Administration	0	0	500	3,877	4,000	9,333
Department of Transportation	10,042	953	10,442	1,221	11,325	1,150
Office of Economic Opportunity	0	7,446	0	5,095	0	11,295
Department of Labor	0	2,839	1,900	3,000	3,100	3,000
Department of Agriculture	3,158	0	3,602	0	3,810	0
National Aeronautics and Space Administration	24	248	58	1,114	58	1,180
Atomic Energy Commission	243	0	159	0	149	0
Other Independent Agencies	212	0	590	0	465	0
Totals	554,614	103,739	659,697	287,644	739,111	518,227

SOURCE: Advisory Commission on Intergovernmental Relations, *Making the Safe Streets Act Work: An Intergovernmental Challenge* (Washington, D.C.: Government Printing Office, 1971).

TABLE 5-5

Federal Outlays for the Reduction of Crime
(in thousands of dollars)

Programs	1969 Actual		1970 Estimate		1971 Estimate	
	Direct	Support	Direct	Support	Direct	Support
Crime research and statistics	9,687	3,756	11,138	15,782	12,779	30,430
Reform of criminal laws	287	59	351	686	298	1,154
Services for prevention of crime	21,572	26,208	25,588	78,197	31,918	154,923
Federal criminal law enforcement	356,225	0	427,624	0	472,823	0
Law enforcement support	5,170	48,569	8,161	130,063	14,717	221,921
Court administration and prosecution	67,502	1,036	80,453	9,089	85,335	25,116
Rehabilitation of offenders	94,171	11,211	106,382	29,555	121,241	56,083
Planning and Coordination of crime reduction programs	0	12,900	0	24,272	0	28,600
Totals	554,614	103,739	659,697	287,644	739,111	518,227

SOURCE: Advisory Commission on Intergovernmental Relations, *Making the Safe Streets Act Work: An Intergovernmental Challenge* (Washington, D.C.: Government Printing Office, 1971).

TABLE 5-6

Federal Outlays for the Reduction of Crime

Program	1969		1970			1971		
	Actual	% of Program Total	Estimate	% Increase	% of Program Total	Estimate	% Increase	% of Program Total
Federal criminal law enforcement	346,225	54	427,624	20	45	472,823	11	38
Law enforcement support	53,739	8	138,224	157	15	236,638	71	19
Services for prevention of crime	47,780	7	103,785	117	11	186,841	80	15
Rehabilitation of offenders	105,382	16	135,937	29	14	177,324	30	14
Court administration and prosecution	68,538	10	89,542	31	9	110,451	23	9
Crime research and statistics	13,443	2	26,920	100	3	43,209	61	3
Planning and coordination of crime reduction programs	12,900	2	24,272	88	3	28,600	18	2
Reform of criminal laws	346	—	1,037	200	—	1,452	40	—
Totals	658,353	100	947,341	44	100	1,257,338	33	100

SOURCE: U.S. Bureau of the Budget, Special Analyses, Budget of the United States, Fiscal Year 1971 (Washington, D.C.: Government Printing Office, 1970), pp. 197-98.

administrator (i.e., mayor or city or county manager type), the legislative body, or if he is elected, to the citizens as a whole. All these represent centers of power to which he owes accountability (or administrative and policy-making allegiance). Such a diffusion of administrative accountability to each respective local power base makes reconciliation between these power centers difficult. "The local ordering of police authority and responsibility introduces the element of parochialism of local orientation, to the resolution of area-wide problems." [23]

Coupled with the parochial distribution of administrative responsibility to local power centers is a wide range of conflicts which arise out of "personal resentment and acrimony between police executives, [and] the disharmony often affects the relationship of field personnel." [24] Loyalty to the organization is part of the character of most police departments. When the average police executive is challenged concerning the persons to whom he feels most responsible, then the typical answer is "to my men." A police chief in the police department of a large eastern city said,

> when all the chips are down, my first loyalty, and my last actions will be taken to protect my men. After all, when you strip all the gold off my hat and take the name plate off my door, what have you got left? I'll tell you—just another cop. That's what I am more than anything else—a cop like all the rest of the men in blue out there. If I don't continue to think of them and defend them against all the other county and state guys and even the feds—then I don't deserve to be sitting here.[25]

The sense of internal commitment relayed in such a statement is communicated to the other officers on the force. An appearance of top-to-bottom loyalty can develop in such a strong manner that, as one author points out, police employees begin to see their role vis-à-vis other police departments, as well as the public, as one of

> doing battle in the name of the chief. A chief's personal dislike for the sheriff or for another chief of police, his resentment toward the policy of another, becomes the dislike and the resentment of many of his subordinates. Often unaware of the subtleties of the dispute, field personnel nevertheless may find themselves acting as the extension of their leader's personality.[26]

---

[23] Misner, "Recent Development in Metropolitan Law Enforcement," p. 506.

[24] Ibid.

[25] From a background interview carried on by the author while conducting a study of an eastern police department.

[26] Misner, "Recent Development in Metropolitan Law Enforcement," p. 506.

The interaction between field personnel of various departments within a metropolitan area is affected by the sense of loyalty they may feel not only toward their chiefs but also toward their departments. Interagency rivalries, jealousies, and personal disputes are compounded by the differences in the quality of the personnel recruited, salaries, the varying levels of training, quality of equipment, and technologies (communication, record keeping, and the like). Such conflicts materialize in a variety of ways. Efforts to cope with crimes which take on a metropolitan-wide aspect, such as chasing speeders, detecting burglary rings, or cracking down on the trafficking of contraband, are often sabotaged by communication systems which transmit on entirely different wavelengths, or by the disparate ability of police departments to pick up a crime in progress. Further conflict may arise when the flight of a criminal from one district into another more competent district of the metropolitan area results in embarrassing the less effective personnel and their chief.

Procedural Conflicts

The various conflicts between police departments extend beyond political, personal, and personnel differences to include the various ways procedures are followed within the same metropolitan region. Practically every area of administrative procedure is implemented in a markedly different way in different parts of the country. However, certain procedural characteristics are commonly in conflict in most metropolitan areas:

General policies
1. recruitment policies
2. proficiency of police personnel
3. cooperativeness of personnel
4. general law enforcement policies

Operations
1. patrol procedures
2. intensity or frequency of patrol
3. quality of investigation

Exchange of information
1. readiness to exchange information
2. accuracy of information
3. willingness to establish central pool of information
4. confidence of privileged communication

Custody of prisoners
1. jail procedures
2. treatment of arrested persons

3. accessibility of arrested persons for interrogation
4. bail procedures
5. release of "floaters" [27]

The various procedures used to recruit and train officers, the quality and comprehensiveness of the techniques of patroling the community, and the quality and methods of incarceration procedures are distinctly different in many metropolitan areas in this country. In short, while there have been substantial strides made to coordinate police procedures in many metropolitan areas (such as setting up regional training institutes, regional and statewide record-keeping systems; multidistrict communication networks; and even the full assumption of police duties by central city municipalities or more efficient counties), these reforms have just begun to lessen the disorganization which is both legal-jurisdictional and procedural.

The drive for governmental reform at the metropolitan-wide or service-basin-wide level has received a significant boost by the increase in regional communication and record-keeping centers. In fact, along with library district consolidation and water district consolidations, one of the most popular multijurisdiction service district experiments is the centralization of certain law enforcement procedures such as communication, records, crime labs, and training. So, while the basic patterns of police service delivery remain somewhat cluttered, there is some consolidation of certain support procedures critical to quality administration of the law enforcement function.

Differences in the Administration of Law and Order

Perhaps no other indicator of the diversity of policy implementation at the local level is as expressive as the type of police behavior exhibited by different local police forces as they administer the unitary law and preserve the social order for all citizens. James Q. Wilson records wide variations in the ways in which police officers carry out their routine law enforcement and order-maintenance functions in eight different types

---

[27] Ibid., p. 507. Misner describes a "floater" as follows: "In police parlance, a "floater" may be given to an arrested person, in effect dismissing the charges against him if he will agree to leave the jurisdiction. Normally given only in minor offenses, the effect upon surrounding areas may, nonetheless, be considerable. The use of "floaters" for alcoholics simply moves the subject to another jurisdiction, and does not hope to affect any rehabilitation."

of metropolitan jurisdictions.[28] Wilson's view attributes the differences in such behavior to certain organizational and legal constraints under which patrolmen work. Such constraints are a product of the administrative style of the chief administrator, the socioeconomic character and size of the community, the resultant size of the police department, or a combination of these.

An example of the varying styles of law enforcement can be seen in the manner in which police departments issue traffic tickets. Wilson discovered that in the case of traffic law, the administrative style and goals of the chief were more salient indicators of the level of law enforcement activity than were the laws themselves, the numbers of people in the area, or the nature of the highways upon which people traveled. For example, two of the police departments he studied served central cities of approximately the same size, same socioeconomic features, and similar street patterns. Yet the police department in one city issued ten times more tickets than did the police department in the other. When he studied the traffic law enforcement of two similar upper-middle class suburbs he found that one issued 50 percent more tickets than the other. When he compared a city in California with a county in New York, he found that while they both exhibited similar highway patterns, the city police issued four times as many tickets as the police of the county.[29] These rather particular studies by Wilson corroborate the finding of John A. Gardiner who, in a comprehensive study of over five hundred cities, found that most differences in traffic law enforcement levels can be attributed to the inducements placed upon police officers by their administrative superiors.[30]

The nature of administrative "decisions" in the areas of traffic law enforcement can in part be attributed to the administrator's decision to create special traffic units whose expressed task is to ferret out and apprehend traffic violators. Further, traffic law enforcement can be more efficient in one department because of the use of technologically sophisticated patrol units armed with radar speed detectors and the like. However, Wilson argues that even when departments with advanced technologies are compared, there are striking differences, and here the differences are attributable to the pressures or inducements placed upon police officers by their superiors to "produce" tickets.[31]

---

[28] James Q. Wilson, *Varieties of Police Behavior: The Management of Law and Order in Eight Communities.* © 1968 by the President and Fellows of Harvard University Press. This section is, in large part, informed by the work of Professor Wilson.

[29] Ibid., p. 96.

[30] John A. Gardiner, *Traffic and the Police: Variations in Law-Enforcement Policy* (Cambridge, Mass.: Harvard University Press, 1969).

[31] Wilson, *Varieties of Police Behavior.*

Wilson points out that such administrative discretion is usually exercised either through a quota system or through informal pressure. Under a quota system (practically no police administrator will formally admit that he uses one), Wilson found that police officers are expected to write anywhere from two tickets a week, per man, to two tickets per man, per hour.

Strong pressure from the chief for all law enforcement officers to enforce the law to the letter can also produce higher levels of service output. Wilson described the situation in two communities as follows:

> When a "reform" police chief came to Syracuse in 1963, he announced that he expected all officers—in and out of the traffic division—to enforce traffic laws. By the end of 1964, ticket production had increased 58 percent and between 1964 and 1965 it increased another 18 percent. After a new chief arrived in Highland Park in the mid-1950's, the number of tickets issued tripled during his first two years in office. Though no quota existed, any officer who "was below the average" for a particular month was called in by the chief and, according to one lieutenant, "had to explain why." [32]

At a more general level of conceptualization, Wilson has attempted to detail the differences in departmental style which affect the enforcement of certain laws. He relies on a well-argued definition of administrative discretion and the extent to which the discretionary style of the chief and the other superiors within a police department can affect the way in which police departments will carry on the police function. Where Misner prefers to term such differences as "attitudes," [33] Wilson sees styles of different departmental behavior emerging. These differences in service delivery are categorized as the "watchman style," the "legalistic style," and the "service style." By "style" Wilson refers to those definitive characteristics of patrolman behavior which become "the style or strategy of the department as a whole because . . . [they are] . . . reinforced by the attitudes and policies of the police administrator." [34]

The Watchman Style.   According to Wilson, the watchman style embodies a preponderant tendency on the part of a police department to use as its operational code a concern for maintaining order, as opposed to strict adherence to law enforcement as the prime characteristic of the police function at the street level. (See pp. 49-53 for a detailed discussion.) Such a style has deep historical roots inasmuch as the first police officials carried on order-maintaining functions under the rubric of the nightwatch

---

[32] Ibid., pp. 97-98.

[33] Misner, "Recent Development in Metropolitan Law Enforcement," p. 507.

[34] Wilson, *Varieties of Police Behavior*, p. 140.

(see chapter 2 for a detailed discussion). Wilson generalizes a description of such departmental style as follows:

> to the extent the administrator can influence the discretion of his men, he does so by allowing them to ignore many common minor violations, especially traffic aand juvenile offenses, to tolerate, though gradually less so, a certain amount of vice and gambling, to use the law more as a means of maintaining order than of regulating conduct, and to judge the requirements of order differently depending on the character of the group in which the infraction occurs. Juveniles are "expected" to misbehave, and thus infractions among this group—unless they are serious or committed by a "wise guy"—are best ignored or treated informally. Negroes are thought to want, and to deserve, less law enforcement because to the police their conduct suggests a low level of public and private morality, an unwillingness to cooperate with the police or offer information, and widespread criminality. Serious crimes, of course, should be dealt with seriously; further, when Negroes offend whites, who, in the eyes of the police, have a different standard of public order, then an arrest must be made. Motorists, unless a departmental administrator wants to "make a record" by giving a few men the job of writing tickets, will often be left alone if their driving does not endanger or annoy others and if they do not resist or insult police authority.[35]

In short, police officers in communities exhibiting the watchman style are ordered to "ignore the 'little stuff' but to 'be tough' where it is important. For example, the police have essentially a 'familial' rather than law enforcement view of juvenile offenders. Their policy is to ignore most infractions ('kids will be kids') and to act *in loco parentis* with respect to those that cannot be ignored: administer a swift kick or a verbal rebuke, have the boy do some chores ('Tom Sawyer justice') or turn him over to his parents for discipline." [36]

In Wilson's analysis, such departments have some common organizational and personnel characteristics. They have minimal requirements for entry to the force, providing low financial incentives for entry and limited wage increments for continuing service to the department. For example, in 1967 the central city of one metropolitan area did not require applicants to have a high school diploma, the chief earned $9,800, and a patrolman $4,800. A six-week recruit training program was instituted by the city, but only after such police training programs were mandated by state law. These organizational and personnel requirements have made the recruitment of quality officers difficult.[37]

---

[35] Ibid., p. 141.

[36] Ibid., p. 145.

[37] Ibid., pp. 140-71.

The results of such a style have been that most police officers are selective in their administration of the laws—especially given the exact group of potential offenders they are dealing with. They are much more likely to take the attitude that one should not rock the boat—the police should support the perceived norms of the community pertaining to potential crimes which are minor or do not appear to offend the community mores. Second, there is little cause to be overly alarmed about the behavior of blacks against blacks. If, on the other hand, black residents act in a way which may be construed as offensive to the authority which the police themselves represent, then strong action will be taken. While this pattern has diminished in its openness, Wilson argues that the watchman style is a highly conducive environment for such behavior.[38]

The Legalistic Style. A police officer exhibiting the legalistic style of police behavior operates under directives which place more importance upon law enforcement than upon order maintenance (see chapter 3, pp. 49-53). The police officer is expected to act in a uniform way which objectively mandates that he strictly interpret the actions of the citizenry within the tenets of law he is pledged to enforce. As a result, such a department

> will issue traffic tickets at a high rate, obtain and arrest a high proportion of juvenile offenders, act vigorously against illicit enterprises, and make a large number of misdemeanor arrests even when, as with petty larceny, the public order has not been breached. The police will act, on the whole, as if there were a single standard of community conduct—that which the law prescribes—rather than different standards for juveniles, Negroes, drunks and the like.[39]

The departments Wilson includes in such a category are usually administered by reform-minded chiefs and are organized in a streamlined fashion, which means the dissolution of old precinct systems and the incorporation of centrally directed patrol units and a complement of special units such as traffic, criminal investigation, internal inspection, crime lab, research and records units, and community relations staffs. The personnel are subject to internal investigations of misconduct, inspections of their equipment and their appearance, and relatively extensive training programs. Due to the diverse organization of units comprising such a structure, police personnel are offered a greater number of jobs and broader job mobility.

---

[38] Ibid., p. 170.

[39] Ibid., p. 172

Such a spirit of law enforcement encourages the use of technological efficiency, planning, and research which produces fact-finding studies.

There are certain consequences of such a style of service delivery which are not always the intended results of such reforms. Any group which feels that it has an inordinate number of contacts with the police (black residents, residents of high-crime areas) often finds the actions of legalist-minded police a source of harrassment. Second, the higher level of police-citizen contacts in legalistic-style serviced cities intensifies the environment in which alleged incidents of police misbehavior or charges of police brutality occur.

> Exacerbating such feelings may be police policies designed to prevent crime, such as aggressive preventive patrol and the preparation of field contact reports on "suspicious" street activity. Taken together, these elements of the legalistic style, even though wholly within the law, based on sound empirical generalizations as to the areas in which crime is most likely to occur and as nondiscriminatory as organizational leadership can make them, may be experienced as harrassment.[40]

The Service Style. The service style of policing a jurisdiction takes on many of the qualities of both the watchman and legalistic styles. Such a style of police service is usually found in communities which are not split dramatically along class or racial lines—they are usually relatively homogeneous communities that are moderately reform-minded. As such, the service style is described as one where "police . . . act as if their task were to estimate the 'market' for police services and to produce a 'product' that meets the demand." [41] In this spirit, Wilson goes on to point out that

> for patrolmen especially, the pace of police work is more leisurely (there are fewer radio messages per tour of duty than in a community with a substantial lower class) and the community is normally peaceful, thus apparent threats to order are more easily detected. Furthermore, the citizenry expects its police officers to display the same qualities as its department store salesmen, local merchants, and public officials—courtesy, a neat appearance, and a deferential manner. Serious matters—burglaries, robberies, assaults—are of course taken seriously and thus "suspicious" persons are carefully watched or questioned. But with regard to minor infractions of the law, arrests are avoided when possible (the rates at which traffic tickets are issued and juveniles referred to Family Court will be much lower than

---

[40] Ibid., p. 191.
[41] Ibid., p. 200.

in legalistic departments) but there will be frequent use of informal, nonarrest sanctions (warnings issued to motorists, juveniles taken to headquarters or visited in their homes for lectures).[42]

It appears from the Wilson study that service style departments are influenced by the opinions and demands of the community. The more affluent the community the more highly regarded will be the demands and opinions of the citizens. For example, in Nassau County, New York, Wilson found that the purpose of such a pattern is aimed at

> keeping the department "small" and close to the people, emphasizing community and public relations, maintaining the best and the shiniest of buildings and equipment, and developing various control procedures that make service a major concern to officers at every rank. And community concerns over some specific law enforcement problem are met, and often anticipated, by the department by creating a specialized unit to deal with it.[43]

Such behavior is carried out by well-trained police officers who, in the case of the Nassau department, work out of precincts and walk beats in the towns of the county. In this case, a large county department (3,200 personnel) has taken over the police function in the towns and villages of the county—a situation which is an exception for county departments within metropolitan areas. The following is an example of how the service style of the county police department in Nassau has successfully overcome some of the fragmentation and overlap of a village and town police forces:

> One village, thinking of asking the NCPD to patrol its area and abandoning its own police force, told the NCPD, as reported by a senior officer who spoke to the local officials, that "They wanted to be sure they had as policemen, men who understood the special problems of a rich community." The NCPD, according to one official, assured them that it would "give them well-screened men who would understand their special needs." [44]

This case clearly spells out the emphasis which the service style places on the special needs of groups and communities. For example, in this well-to-do village, serious emphasis may be placed upon burglary detection techniques and less serious attention may be addressed to arrests for drunkenness. In low-income sectors of the community where high-risk crime activities often occur, the procedures of "stop and chat" may be

---

[42] Ibid., p. 201.

[43] Ibid., p. 203.

[44] Ibid., p. 204.

quite prevalent where the investigative stopping of citizens on the street of the well-to-do village may be an infrequent activity.

The consequences of such a style are less evident than those of the other styles. It has been alleged, though proof is lacking, that such a system of justice leads to lenient policing of notables in the community and relatively strict policing of those less well known. Further, the amount of criticism by black groups of such departments is less vocal than it has been against police departments exhibiting either the watchman or legalistic styles of police service delivery. However, this may be the case because such departments have much less contact with nonwhite minorities than do the police departments utilizing other styles.[45]

Conclusion. The differentiation in the quality and practice of the police function is not only the product of intrametropolitan spread and diversity of governmental jurisdictions and the intergovernmental relations of the federal, state, and local governments interested in the administration of justice; it can also be attributed to the inducements of the administrative superior and the institutionalized styles of each of the departments as a whole. The structure and administration of the police function are examples of much of the jurisdictional and functional confusion which attends the provision of public services in the metropolitan areas in general. To this end, the study of the police function, while in and of itself a valuable process, also has a more general heuristic value as well.

Fiscal Spread and Diversity

Governmental fragmentation and overlap is accompanied by spread and diversity of fiscal efforts of local governments within the metropolis. Such patterns of government partition not only the population but also the financial resources which support service delivery. As was discussed in the previous section, the extent of service disparities in the police function and other public services can, in part, be attributed to state directives set forth in constitutions and statutes which prescribe the types and re-sponsibilities of local government. The multiplicity of governments and the service loads assigned to them by the state are important determinants of the patterns of local government finance. Coupled with the impact of such service designations upon fiscal patterns in the metropolis are the patterns of social migration into and out of the central city and its surrounding governmental jurisdictions. Such migration patterns result in

---

[45] Ibid., pp. 215-26.

intrametropolitan clusters of high-cost and low-cost citizenries within the various jurisdictions. While there are extremely poor suburban communities and there are very distinct patterns of socioeconomic disparities among suburban residents,[46] the most common pattern is one of a concentration of high-cost citizenry in the core or central cities relative to the residential composition and service needs of suburban residents. Such residential disparities are accompanied by fiscal disparity between the central city and the outside central city area.[47] One study argues that "the adverse fiscal situation of the core city is reflected in higher tax efforts and in distorted functional distribution of expenditures." [48]

Perhaps this statement is an accurate summation of the metropolitan condition with regard to what has been termed "the fiscal crisis." The effect of the assignment of unequal service loads upon differing types of local governments coupled with the shifting patterns of socially, economically, and politically disparate residents and industries has resulted in substantial diversity in the revenue-gathering abilities and expenditure patterns of local governments within metropolitan areas. This part of the metropolitan condition cannot be ignored by those concerned with understanding metropolitanism or with studying the police function.

The remainder of this chapter will discuss the nature of fiscal spread and diversity and the effect such patterns of metropolitanism have upon the delivery of police services. We will first review briefly the nature of central city-outside central city fiscal disparities and the influence of the special district upon such patterns of disparity. Then we will turn to a discussion of the patterns of police expenditures in an attempt to demonstrate how the financial efforts of local governments in pursuit of law and order stand as an example of this important metropolitan pattern.

Fiscal Disparities within the Metropolis

A person moves out of one community and into another one for various reasons. Certain communities appear to have the ability to pull residents to them, and others seem to suffer from conditions which seem to push residents to other places. Such is the basic assertion of the push-pull

---

[46] David C. Perry, "The Suburb as a Model for Neighborhood Control," in *Neighborhood Control in the 1970s: Politics Administration and Citizen Participation*, ed. H. George Frederickson (New York: Chandler Intext, 1973), pp. 85-99.

[47] Campbell and Sacks, *Metropolitan America*, and Roy W. Bahl and Robert E. Firestine, "Urban-Suburban Migration Patterns and Metropolitan Fiscal Structures," mimeographed (Paper delivered at the annual meeting of the American Political Science Association, Washington, D.C., 1973).

[48] Ibid., p. 1.

statements of urban and rural mobility. Those communities which have a tendency to attract residents do so because they provide a desirable racial or ethnic mix, religious composition, or population size and growth rate: often they represent income advantages, occupational opportunities, and educational opportunities.[49] Other studies have added to this list such characteristics as sex, age composition,[50] family structure, and regional location.[51] Along with such socioeconomic determinants of intra- and intermetropolitan mobility is an argument first put forth by the economist Charles Tiebaut. Tiebaut has argued that certain fiscal determinants also affect the perceptions of the local residents and can account for their residential preferences. The Tiebaut thesis makes the assumption that the metropolitan resident is not merely driven to move by the social, economic, ethnic, racial or occupational drives but also has certain preferential patterns of purchase of public goods which can be likened to those of a customer entering a supermarket.[52] Using Bahl and Firestine's concise description of the model:

> each prospective consumer-resident shops around the metropolitan area until finding the community that offers a tax-expenditure package which corresponds most closely to his own preference function for public services. He then "votes with his feet" by moving to that community.[53]

Hence, without dismissing the importance of the other socioeconomic factors affecting the residential selection patterns of metropolitan residents, it will be argued here that local financial activities affect patterns of metropolitan growth, spread, and diversity as well.

As was discussed in the first chapter, such fiscal patterns are part of a general characteristic of metropolitan areas which can be loosely termed economic spread and diversity. The movement throughout a metropolitan area of various sectors of its economic base, as the industries attempt to satisfy requirements of labor markets, consumer markets, space for industrial site reconstruction, or position of proximity to external support

---

[49] James W. Simmons, "Changing Residence in the City: A Review of Intra Urban Mobility," *The Geographical Review* 58, 4 (October 1968): 622-51.

[50] Karl and Alma Teauber, "White Migration and Socio-Economic Differences Between Cities and Suburbs," *American Sociological Review* 29 (October 1963): 718-29.

[51] James D. Tarver and William R. Gurley, "The Relationship of Selected Variables with County Net Migration Rates in the United States, 1950 to 1960" *Rural Sociology* 30, 1 (March 1965): 3-13.

[52] Charles Tiebaut, "A Pure Theory of Local Expenditures," *Journal of Political Economy* 64 (October 1956): 416-24.

[53] Bahl and Firestine, "Urban-Suburban Migration Patterns," p. 3.

services,[54] is an attempt by these industries to maximize their economies of scale. A significant percentage of secondary and tertiary sector economic activities (or manufacturing and service industries) have left the central city as have great numbers of relatively affluent white residents. Such movements have depleted the tax resources and forced the central city (the traditional local government assigned with a maximum service load) to take on a reciprocal and intense dual responsibility of serving low-income, high-cost clusters of residents, with either a declining or slowly growing tax base.

The relative affluence gained by the out-migration of both residents and industries to the outside central city jurisdictions creates varying financial patterns within the metropolitan areas.[55] The most dramatic pattern in terms of tax bases, expenditures, and intergovernmental aid can generally be found in the fiscal differences between central cities or core municipalities and the outside central city governments. Practically every major study of the nation's largest SMSAs agrees that the spread and diversity of fiscal resources within the metropolis is one which finds the core cities in a relatively declining position of fiscal solvency *vis-à-vis* their surrounding suburban governments. The central city is bound by its general service provision assignment as an incorporated municipality to provide more services than most of its suburban counterparts. Further, the central city must presently be concerned with a higher proportion of high-cost citizens whose demands are more extreme than those of the surrounding areas's citizens. To meet the needs of such citizens the city must mobilize its unhealthy resource base via the traditional taxing and bond raising procedures available to such governments. Conversely, the outside central city has been blessed, in large part, by significant numbers of low-cost, high-income citizens, and with increases in the share of the manufacturing and service sectors of the metropolitan economic base. These growing components of suburbanization serve as sources from which to raise increased revenue to provide the range of public services assigned selectively and otherwise undertaken by the different types of governments which dot the outside central city landscape.

Differing tax burdens are also placed on citizens living in the central city or the outside central city. For the thirty-seven largest metropolitan areas, the local tax burden of central city residents amounts to 7.6 percent of personal income, while the same burden in the outside central city

---

[54] Edgar M. Hoover and Raymond Vernon, *Anatomy of a Metropolis* (Garden City, N.Y.: Doubleday, Anchor Edition, 1962).

[55] Roy W. Bahl, "Public Policy and the Urban Fiscal Problem: Piecemeal vs. Aggregate Solutions," *Land Economics* 46, 1 (February 1970): 41-50.

area registers only 5.6 percent of personal income.[56] Such data is suggestive of an unequal tax burden placed upon residents of the central city relative to those of the outside central city inasmuch as median family income in the city is 18 percent less than such income levels evidenced by metropolitan residents living in the outside central city area. Another study reveals further evidence of an increasing burden placed upon the central city resident as compared to the burden of the outside central city resident:

> in 25 metropolitan areas for which comparable 1961 and 1966 data are available, assessed values increased 63 percent in the suburbs as contrasted with only 24 percent in central cities. In the same vein, the growth rates for alternative non-property taxes (retail sales, employment, and personal income taxes) were all lower in central cities than in suburbs.[57]

Such a rising level of taxes for central city residents, supported by slowly growing values of property as well as alternative forms of taxable resources, as compared to the position of many suburban residents, certainly places the service-burdened and resource-poor central city and its residents under an extreme strain.

Let us return to the tendency of states to assign special district privileges, or at least limited general service provision loads, to outside central city municipalities and counties. The most common special district is the school district. Such a jurisdictional delineation of the education function results in a spending pattern which finds the incorporated core municipalities spending far less per capita on education than the governments in the outside central cities. While this lower level of spending in the core municipalities is more a function of the larger number of public services within cities which force government officials to stretch the tax dollar over more areas of need, the conditions of jurisdictional fragmentation emphasize central city-outside central city disparities, in support for public services.

The central city raises more taxes and spends more money for noneducational services than do the governments of the outside central city. Further, the same pattern can be seen in the patterns of aggregate intergovernmental aid—64 percent of state and federal aid to the suburbs goes to education, and conversely, 64 percent of the aid to the cities goes to direct noneducational public services. (See table 1-7 in chapter 1 for the aggregate figures.)

As we indicated earlier in this chapter, the police function is quite different in its jurisdictional definition from the education function. Rarely

---

[56] ACIR, *State and Local Finances: Significant Features, 1967-1970* (Washington, D.C.: Government Printing Office, 1969), p. 68.

[57] Bahl and Firestine, "Urban-Suburban Migration Patterns," p. 6.

is the police function administered through a single-purpose government. As table 5-7 demonstrates, thirty-seven of the largest metropolitan areas in the country demonstrate a significant difference in aggregate expenditures for law enforcement between central cities and outside central cities. In fact, 72.3 percent of the total amount spent on law enforcement in

TABLE 5-7

CC-OCC Expenditures for Law Enforcement, 1967

	SMSA (000)	CC (000)	OCC (000)
Los Angeles-Long Beach	$ 115,651	$ 72,439	$ 43,212
San Bernardino-Riverside-Ontario	9,569	4,735	834°
San Diego	12,683	8,506	4,177
San Francisco-Oakland	42,223	27,782	14,441
Denver	9,903	7,000	2,903
Washington, D.C.-Maryland-Virginia	32,159	27,404	4,755
Miami	15,812	8,367	7,445°
Tampa-St. Petersburg	8,497	5,805	2,692
Atlanta	9,951	6,012	3,939
Chicago	114,479	92,137	22,342
Indianapolis, Indiana	7,644	6,776	868
Louisville, Kentucky-Indiana	6,428	4,545	1,883
New Orleans	8,854	7,559	1,295
Baltimore	29,769	25,152	4,617
Boston	43,281	19,563	23,718
Detroit	54,040	34,911	16,129
Minneapolis-St. Paul	15,446	9,876	5,570
Kansas City, Missouri-Kansas	12,696	9,101	3,595
St. Louis, Missouri-Illinois	26,274	19,381	6,893
Newark	31,532	15,876	15,656°
Paterson-Clifton-Pasaic	18,135	4,676	13,459°
Buffalo, New York	16,494	10,884	5,610
New York, New York	268,652	268,652	52,215°
Cincinnati, Ohio-Kentucky-Indiana	13,519	8,188	6,202
Cleveland, Ohio	26,042	17,048	8,994
Columbus, Ohio	7,607	6,473	1,134
Dayton, Ohio	5,953	3,352	2,601
Portland, Oregon-Washington	9,240	7,662	1,578
Philadelphia, Pennsylvania-New Jersey	60,162	44,598	15,564
Pittsburgh, Pennsylvania	24,109	11,182	12,927
Providence, R.I.-Massachusetts	8,938	5,522	3,416
Dallas, Texas	13,441	10,075	3,366
Houston, Texas	14,133	11,867	2,266
San Antonio, Texas	6,063	5,081	982
Seattle-Everett, Washington	12,829	10,272	2,557
Milwaukee, Wisconsin	21,479	15,729	5,750
Total	1,192,059	862,474	330,455
Percentage spent by area	100.0%	72.3%	27.7%

°As defined in 1967.

SOURCE: This table is compiled from a series of volumes of data assembled by the U.S. Bureau of Census (Washington, D.C.: Government Printing Office, 1967-1969).

these metropolitan areas in 1967 was spent in the central city while only 27.7 percent of such expenditures occurred in the outside central city.

In table 5-8, a more complete breakdown is given of the fiscal importance placed upon the police function as compared to other non-education functions by various types of communities within one of these major metropolitan areas (Milwaukee, Wisconsin). More than 30 percent of the local operating budget of the central city of Milwaukee is spent on the police function. This is a third again as high as the next most significant sector of the operating budget (health and sanitation). By comparison, expenditures for police in the immediately adjacent urban suburbs rank second to highway expenditures; in the incorporated non-urban suburbs it ranks third behind highways and general governmental expenditures; and in the incorporated areas it ranks fourth, just ahead of fire and recreation expenditures. Hence the metropolitan resident of Milwaukee, depending upon where he lives in the SMSA, can expect widely varying fiscal outlays for police service.

The police service, recalling the Tiebaut, Bahl and Firestine arguments, is packaged in widely diverse metropolitan services. The nature of the local government makes a significant difference and can be described in terms of the fiscal pattern it projects through its packaging of public services. While there are no hard and fast correlations between the success rate of fiscal outlay and the diminution of crime, there is evidence which suggests that more money is spent in areas where there are higher crime rates. For example, in Milwaukee, the further one goes from the central city the less money that is spent on police activities, and, as of 1969, 240 percent more crimes occurred in the central city area of Milwaukee than occurred in the outside central city area. The Milwaukee metropolitan area mirrors metropolitan areas which exceed one million in population. Of those metropolitan areas in the country which compose approximately 15 percent of the total population of the nation, the central city experienced 240 percent more crime than the outside central city areas.

The fiscal outlays and service programs in law enforcement of the central cities are relatively more extensive than outside city efforts. In general, the city experiences more crime and is less healthy fiscally than its outside central city area. Outside central city fiscal patterns support the image of well-educated children and clean crime-free suburbs. This is borne out in the general findings that fully 64 percent of state and federal aid to the suburbs goes to education. Further, the vast proportion of the remainder of state aid goes to highways and health care, with some states adding a good measure of support for public welfare where it is a service function assigned to the counties. Here again we see a preference for public services outside the central city which are highly subsidized by intergovernmental

TABLE 5-8

Shares of Major Operating Expenditures in the Milwaukee SMSA, 1966
(Noneducation only)

	General Government	Police	Fire	Health and Sanitation	Highways	Recreation	Total
Central city	14.6%	30.5%	16.1%	20.1%	14.7%	3.9%	100.0%
Urban area suburbs	19.4	20.8	13.0	13.2	29.4	3.8	100.0
Incorporated: outside urban area	26.0	14.8	10.7	11.2	29.5	6.1	100.0
Unincorporated: outside urban area	29.4	5.6	11.9	4.3	46.7	1.3	100.0

SOURCE: Advisory Commission on Intergovernmental Relations, *Fiscal Balance in the American Federal System, Vol. II: Metropolitan Fiscal Disparities* (Washington, D.C.: Government Printing Office, 1967), p. 301.

aid. Until recently, police service has not been a highly aided function, nor has crime been a significant outside central city concern, and so has not ranked high on the preference ordering of the suburbanite.

The Role of Federal and State Governments

While much has been made in recent years of this fiscal mismatch of resources and needs which have accompanied the social migration and economic spread in the metropolis, there are other fiscal patterns to be considered as well. Either because of the rural bias of many state legislatures or because of the complex and costly housekeeping duties placed upon state governments, the states have avoided addressing many of the growing and politically sensitive public service problems of local governments.[58]

Until the 1960s, the states and the federal government were little concerned with financially aiding local law enforcement institutions. With the increase in crime, the growth of racial violence, the dislodging appearance of new racial urbanities, and the spread of organized crime, a concommitant increase in interest in the law enforcement function materialized. In 1965, President Johnson created the President's Commission on Law Enforcement and Administration of Justice. One of the results of the report of this Commission was the enactment of the Omnibus Crime Control and Safe Streets Act of 1968. Title I of this act comprised the federal governments' first comprehensive grant-in-aid program to the reluctant states and beleaguered local governments in the areas of law enforcement and criminal justice administration. It also represented one of the first major attempts by the federal government to institute block grant funding to states and localities.

In an attempt to force the reluctant states to start to coordinate and support the local law enforcement function more actively, each state received a planning grant from the Law Enforcement Assistant Agency (LEAA) with the express purpose of creating a law enforcement planning agency. The primary responsibility of these agencies was to draw up comprehensive law enforcement plans for their respective states. The plans were subject to the approval of the LEAA, and the results of such approval could be the award of federal grants earmarked for specific programs or discretionary in nature.

In 1968, the funding by the federal government was primarily for planning these agencies. Special grants were given to forty states for riot control and another set of special grants was awarded for studies concerning organized crime, the need for police equipment, and other areas of concern.

---

[58] See the classic book on federalism by Martin, *Cities in the Federal System.*

By 1971, the total of federal grants to the states had topped $1.2 billion, fully 91 percent more than the funds awarded in 1969, and one-third more money than was spent by the federal government in 1970. It is estimated that by the mid-1970s the federal government will be spending more than double what it spent in 1971. With the increase in funds has come an increase in the purposes for such grants. Beyond the discretionary funding, states and localities now receive funds in twelve general categories:

1. Riots and civil disorders control.
2. Upgrading law enforcement (including training, salary increases, career development).
3. Detection and apprehension.
4. Crime prevention (including public education).
5. Correction and rehabilitation (including probation and parole).
6. Juvenile delinquency prevention and control.
7. Prosecution, court, and law reform.
8. Community relations.
9. Organized crime control.
10. Research and development.
11. Construction.
12. Crime statistics and information.[59]

These state planning agencies have acted more as facilitators of these grants to regions and localities within the states than as new centralized agencies of law enforcement and criminal justice administration. The average size of such an agency is relatively small—only 9.3 professional staff members.[60] Hence, while federal aid has been offered to states in an attempt to lead them towards a centralized coordination of planning for law enforcement and the administration of justice, the states' efforts remain disorderly. The state planning agencies are weak due to the smallness of their staffs and the transience of the political elite who control the supervisory boards of most of these agencies. The result is that many of the federal funds for law enforcement are fast becoming parcels of political patronage in many states, comprehensive planning requirements notwithstanding. Unless the federal government and regional councils of governments review grant applications carefully, the federal grants and state and local contributions will be dispersed in a manner which may provide more money to various police activities but which, at the same time, does not guarantee that the disparities of the metropolis will be considered and relieved any more than they have been in the past.

---

[59] This part of the discussion is taken from the ACIR, *Making the Safe Streets Act Work.*

[60] Ibid.

The People and the Police 6

The focus now shifts from macro-level considerations to a street-level assessment of police in the metropolis. Most contemporary studies of the police focus on the context in which the city police operate or the experiences of police which reveal their personal behavior and professional stance. Within this context, sociologists like Jerome Skolnick, Michael Banton, Jonathan Rubinstein, and Albert Reiss and political scientists such as James Wilson have recently expanded upon the tradition of exploring the arena in which the policeman operates as described by William Westley.[1] These studies primarily concern the perceptions of the police officer and the efficiency with which he provides his service,[2] his "working personality," [3] the interactions between the client and the police officer,[4] and the station house environment in which he works.[5]

---

[1] William A. Westley, *Violence and the Police: A Sociological Study of Law, Custom and Morality* (Cambridge, Mass.: M.I.T. Press, 1970).

[2] Albert J. Reiss, Jr., *Public Perceptions and Recollections About Crime, Law Enforcement and Criminal Justice*, Field Survey III: Studies in Crime and Law Enforcement in Major Metropolitan Areas, vol. I, section II of the President's Commission on Law Enforcement and the Administration of Justice (Washington, D.C.: Government Printing Office, 1967). See also a recently published study by Bernard Cohen and Jan M. Chaiken, *Police Background Characteristics and Performance* (Lexington, Mass.: Lexington Books, 1973); and Michael Banton, *The Policeman and the Community* (New York: Basic Books, 1964).

[3] Jerome H. Skolnick, *Justice Without Trial: Law Enforcement in Democratic Society* (New York: John Wiley, 1967). See also James Q. Wilson, *Varieties of Police Behavior: The Management of Law and Order in Eight Communities* (Cambridge, Mass.: Harvard University Press, 1968).

[4] Reiss, *Public Perceptions and Recollections*. See also Jonathan Rubinstein, *City Police* (New York: Farrar, Straus, and Giroux, 1973).

[5] Rubinstein, *City Police*, and Skolnick, *Justice Without Trial*, present compelling treatments.

The work of these scholars does not exhaust the more recent literature on police, but it is indicative of a change in the academic approach to the study of police. For years the Westley analysis was the only major study of police practice and behaviors drawn from the realities of the street. Most other treatments were antiseptic discussions of police structures and idealized prescriptions of what the police officer should be.[6] Other than a few ventures by social scientists into the behavior of different parts of police departments, most of the literature of police was directed toward training police recruits, apologizing for police practices,[7] or criticizing police practices.[8]

With the exception of scholars such as Wilson, Skolnick, and Banton, the intensifying focus on the street-level activities of police was probably spurred by the revolts and riots of the 1960s.[9] It became dramatically clear that the environment and behavior of police had a significant impact not only on the crime rate and the order of a city, but also on the very survival of cities. That certain actions of the lowest level bureaucrat in the criminal justice hierarchy could affect the functions of the system and the whole social economic and political fabric of a community was indelibly imprinted upon the consciousness of practitioners and scholars alike.

The complex of multiple situations confronting the metropolitan police officer as he strives to serve his clientele; the limited and stereotypical patterns of preparation which officers undergo in order to serve such contemporary complexities; and the political and social pressures which divide and often fracture the modern American metropolis are brought

---

[6] For example, see O. W. Wilson, *Police Administration*, 2nd ed. (New York: McGraw-Hill, 1963). Also see O. W. Wilson, ed., *Parker on Police* (Springfield, Ill.: Charles C. Thomas, 1956). For a representative discussion of the general administrative duties of a department as well as the special tasks required of individual policemen, see Raymond E. Clift, *Police and Public Safety* (Cincinnati: W. H. Anderson, 1963).

[7] Representative of books written to justify the policeman's position is one by Herbert T. Klein, *The Police: Damned If They Do—Damned If They Don't* (New York: Crown, 1968).

[8] For characteristic criticism of the police, see Ernest Jerome Hopkins, *Our Lawless Police: A Study of the Unlawful Enforcement of the Law* (New York: Viking, 1931); Fred J. Cook, *The Corrupted Land: The Social Morality of Modern America* (New York: Macmillan, 1966); Ralph Lee Smith, *The Tarnished Badge: A Factual Report on the Police Scandals That Have Shocked American Cities* (New York: Thomas Y. Crowell, 1965); and Albert Deutsch, *The Trouble With Cops* (London: Arco, 1955).

[9] Robert M. Fogelson, "From Resentment to Confrontation: The Police, the Negroes and the Outbreak of the Nineteen Sixties Riots," *Political Science Quarterly* 83, 2 (June 1968): 217.

together on the streets where the beat patrolmen practice their designated profession. The experiences and environments in which the police officer finds himself serve at times as a "rorschach" of the diverse maladies and social cleavages which afflict the metropolis of the 1970s.

Facing the police officer in the performance of his duties is the social spread and diversity of the metropolis. The various social and economic characteristics of the residents of metropolitan areas are measures of the variety of clientele groups the police must serve and satisfy. The attitudes, values, and experiences of this diverse clientele of the metropolis are the raw material with which the police officer must work. Conversely, such attitudes toward and experiences with the police are indicators of the satisfaction levels of the various city sectors with police service. Finally, the attitudes, frustrations and station-house environment of the patrolman in the city determine, in part, his response to his environment.

Social Spread and Diversity

The patterns of social spread and diversity of the metropolitan areas of the country are ones of relative affluence and whiteness in the suburbs and relative poverty (or at least significantly lower incomes compared to the suburbs) and increasing minority residency in the central city. These patterns of residency reflect increasing numbers of high-cost relatively poor citizens in the central city, while the outside central city areas have increasing portions of low-cost relatively affluent residents. The emphasis here and in the previous section of this chapter is on (1) the heterogeneity of the central city compared to the more homogeneous outside central city and (2) the high-cost nature of central city residents who need a wide range of public services such as welfare, medical services, special education, and extraordinary police services. In general, those who have moved to the outside central city are white and have taken higher incomes and higher levels of educational achievement from the central city to communities with selective services funded at levels which are not as high (except for education) as those found in the central city.[10]

The information displayed in table 6-1 can be viewed as a highly generalized description of the particular social and economic diversity in evidence as one travels the streets of the metropolis. These characteristics

---

[10] See the last section of the previous chapter for a discussion of this characteristic of metropolitanism.

TABLE 6-1

Characteristics of the Metropolitan Population, 1970

Characteristic	Total (243 SMSAs)	Central City	OCC Urban	Rural
Population	139,418,047	63,789,524	59,211,445	16,417,078
Percent/area	100.0%	45.75%	42.47%	11.78%
White	114,975,718	46,022,928	53,811,328	15,141,462
Percent of area	82.47%	72.15%	90.88%	92.23%
Non white	24,442,329	17,766,596	5,400,117	1,275,616
Percent of area	17.53%	27.85%	9.12%	7.77%
Black	16,749,356	13,126,084	2,794,748	828,529
	12.21%	20.58%	4.72%	5.05%
Spanish heritage	7,692,973	4,640,512	2,605,369	447,092
	5.52%	7.27%	4.40%	2.72%
Income				
Median family income				
Total	$10,474	$ 9,507	$11,586	$9,971 /$9,107[1]
White	11,051	10,426	11,829	$10,096
Black	6,832	6,790	7,542	5,186
Spanish heritage	7,834	7,185	9,282	6,670
Families with income below poverty level				
Percentage share of families by area	100.00%	59.0%	28.2%	12.8%
Percent of total families	8.5	11.0	5.6	9.1
Percent of white families	5.9	6.7	4.6	7.6
Percent of black families	24.5	24.5	21.1	36.6
Percent of Spanish heritage families	18.7	21.4	12.6	26.5
Age				
Percent under 18	24.15	31.92	35.48	38.42 /35.46[2]
Percent over 65	9.25	10.76	7.97	7.30 /10.3[3]
Median age	28.0	28.8	27.4	26.3 /31.4[4]
Education				
Median school years completed				
Total population	12.2	12.0	12.3	12.1/11.4[5]
Black	10.1	10.2	10.4	8.0
Spanish heritage	10.2	9.7	11.4	8.2
Employment				
Total employed	56,444,025	26,425,670	23,876,403	6,141,952
Total unemployed	2,409,680	1,251,906	910,938	246,836
Percent unemployed	4.2%	4.7%	3.8%	4.0%
Percent white	3.2	3.0	3.3	3.6
Percent black	6.8	6.9	6.3	6.2
Percent Spanish heritage	6.4	6.5	6.3	6.8

[1]Median family income for all families living in metropolitan rural non-farm (above the slash) and rural farm (below the slash) areas.
[2]Percentage of all those under 18 years living in metropolitan rural non-farm (above the slash) and rural farm (below the slash) areas.
[3]Percentage of all those over 65 years living in metropolitan rural non-farm (above the slash) and rural farm (below the slash) areas.
[4]Median age of all those living in metropolitan non-farm (above the slash) and rural farm (below the slash) areas.
[5]Median number of school years completed by all those living in metropolitan non-farm (above the slash) areas.
SOURCE: U.S., Bureau of the Census, Census of Population, *General Social and Economic Statistics: United States Summary*, vol. C (Washington, D.C.: Government Printing Office, 1972).

eventually become the humanly charged environment of the police officer in his everyday dealings with citizens. They operate as a baseline from which to start translating the patterns of metropolitanism into a vehicle which can be used to understand the police function. Thus a brief discussion will be undertaken of central city-outside central city differentials and of intra-central city characteristics.

Population

The data on population in table 6-1 demonstrate the magnitude of the shift of metropolitan population from the central city to the outside central city. The most populated sector of the outside central city is the rapidly urbanizing suburban ring which contains 78 percent of all those living outside the central city. In fact, there is only a 4.5 million person differential between the population of this urbanized surrounding area and the population of the central city.

The distinctions between the central city and the sectors of the outside central city become more pronounced, however, on examination of the racial characteristics of their respective populations. The central city is decidedly more nonwhite than the urban or rural metropolitan surroundings. Almost 80 percent of the blacks living in the metropolis reside in the central city and 60 percent of the Spanish heritage residents who live in metropolitan areas of this country live in the central city. Consequently 27 percent of the central city population is nonwhite compared to 8.8 percent nonwhite residency in the outside central city.

Income

From table 6-1 it is evident that the most prosperous sectors of the metropolitan areas of the United States are the outside central city nonfarm areas (urban and rural). In all of these areas, the central city and the rural farm area included, the median family income of whites is the most important component in pushing up overall income figures. In fact, as table 6-2 demonstrates, only in the urban fringe of the central city does any group of nonwhite families (Spanish heritage families) begin to generate enough income to begin to approximate the income of comparable white families. Generally speaking, this table demonstrates that black metropolitan residents are still the poorest racial component of the metropolis. These figures represent an increase of approximately 9 percent over comparable patterns of ten years ago. However, the stark reality of an income difference of significant magnitude persists: a black family living in the metropolis is four times as likely to be below the poverty level (mid-1960s income of $3,553 for a family of four) as a white family; and a family of Spanish heritage is three times as likely to be below the poverty level as a white family (see table 6-1). More recent figures comparing the ratio of black to white incomes nationally since 1969 indicate a decline in the ratios set forth in table 6-2.[11] While it is indeed too early to predict, some scholars are beginning to moan in private that 1969 might have been the highwater mark, for at least a few years, in the battle of nonwhite families to close the income gap.

TABLE 6-2

Black and Spanish Heritage Family Incomes° as a
Percentage of White Family Income, 1969°°

	SMSA Total	Central City	Outside Central City	
			Urban	Rural
Black	61.8%	65.1%	63.7%	51.3%
Spanish heritage	70.8	68.9	78.4	66.0

°Median Family Income
°°For further discussion of the statistics found in this table and how they differ from other census statistics see David C. Perry "Faking it and Making it with the U.S. Bureau of the Census: A Research Note." Austin: The University of Texas, 1974. Mimeographed.
SOURCE: U.S. Bureau of Census, *Census of Population, General Social and Economic Characteristics: United States Summary*, Volume C (Washington, D.C.: Government Printing Office, 1972).

The disparities resulting from metropolitan spread and diversity become more apparent when reviewing the statistics which describe incomes of those living below the poverty level. There are nearly three million families living below this level in the metropolitan areas at the present time. These families comprise 8.5 percent of all metropolitan families, with the central cities having the largest number of families at or below the poverty level (11.0 percent of all central city families). More importantly, approximately six out of every ten poor metropolitan families live in the central city. Hence the city contains the largest share of potential high-cost citizens relative to the poverty load found among outside central city urban and rural communities. In the outside central city, where the populations of

---

[11] Incomes for all black families have dropped from 61 percent white income in 1969 to 59 percent in 1972. These figures were computed before the significant down-turn of the economy generated by the energy-related issues of 1973. U.S., Bureau of Commerce, *The Social and Economic Status of the Black Population in the United States, 1972* (Washington, D.C.: Government Printing Office, 1973), p. 17.

blacks and Spanish heritage residents is decidedly lower, from 21.1 to
37.6 percent of the black families are living on an income below the
poverty level compared to from 2.6 percent to 7.6 percent of the white
families. Again, only in the case of Spanish heritage families living on
the urban fringe do the ratios of nonwhite families to white families
seem to dip a bit; even so, the percentage of Spanish families living below
the poverty level is nearly three times as great as that of white families
in the same situation.

Age

With the exception of rural farm areas, the residents of the outside
central city areas are younger than the residents of the central city. This
is accounted for by the better than 6.8 million residents of the central
city who are over the age of 65. They represent 10.76 percent of the
total central city population and this is another indication of the presence
of potential high users of costly social services in the central city. These
residents exhibit diminished capacities to pay for these services due to
age and retirement.

Education

Although the lowest level of educational attainment is found among
the residents of the rural farm area, the black and Spanish heritage residents
of the metropolis are clearly in a substandard educational position *vis-à-vis*
the total metropolitan population. The level of educational attainment
for minority nonwhites is below high school equivalency in every area
of the metropolis. The central city has the second lowest level of educational attainment of all sectors in the metropolis, and it also has by far
the highest level of racial minorities and the second lowest level of educational attainment by these residents. The continuing problems of specialized
and costly education and post-school training remain a significant issue
in the central cities of SMSAs.

Employment

As shown by table 6-1, overall in the metropolis the unemployment
rate for Spanish residents is two times that of whites and the black rate
is slightly more than two times that of whites. In the central city, the
disparity remains the same for the Spanish heritage labor force and is
even greater between black and white workers (the unemployment rate
among black central city dwellers is 230 percent of white unemployment).

In the outside central regions, the disparities are not as great as those found in the central city but they are still considerable.

Crime

One of the most familiar reasons[12] given by central city residents considering a move to the suburbs is that they do not feel safe in the city any more. The only major study conducted to test the reality or myth of such an assertion is the study of the President's Commission on Law Enforcement and Administration of Justice entitled *Criminal Victimization in the United States: A Report of a National Survey*.[13] This study cataloged the experiences of 10,000 families in the United States and discovered that the threat of criminal violence is greater for those in the central city than those in the suburbs or nonmetropolitan areas (see table 6-3). However, Part I crimes (as designated by the FBI Uniform Crime Index) such as larceny and vehicle theft are more prevalent in the suburbs. Part II crimes such as petty theft and malicious destruction of property are more often reported in the suburbs than in the central city.

The most recent data gathered by the FBI for its Uniform Crime Reports demonstrate that even the occurrence of violent crime is increasing in the suburbs. As pointed out in chapter 4, large outside central city suburbs demonstrated the most dramatic increases in such crimes as murder (up 11 percent as compared to an increase of 4 percent in the central cities), and rape (up 19 percent in the suburbs as compared to a 10 percent increase in the central cities. The crime rate data gathered for the President's Commission in the mid-1960s and these patterns of occurrence of violent crime for 1972 indicate that violent crimes against persons and crimes against property are becoming a common part of suburban life in the same way that they have long been part of living in the city.

The Central City:
Diversity
and Disparities

Such data on social disparities and crime rates, are, in the final analysis, data of the street. The people who are represented collectively by these data live in houses and apartments on the streets of the suburbs and the cities. The crimes occur on the streets and in the homes throughout the

---

[12] For a discussion of various reasons of intrametropolitan migration, see chapter 5.

[13] Philip H. Ennis, *Criminal Victimization in the United States: A Report of a National Survey* (Washington, D.C.: Government Printing Office, 1967).

TABLE 6-3

Crime Rates by Metropolitan Sector, 1965
(Per 100,000 Population)

Crime	Central Parts of Metropolitan Areas	Suburban Parts of Metropolitan Areas	Non-Metropolitan Areas
Part I Total	2,860	2,347	1,267
Homicide	0	0	8
Forcible rape	83	38	8
Robbery	207	95	0
Aggravated assault	293	286	110
Burglary	1,335	839	727
Larceny ($50+)	704	810	346
Vehicle theft	238	279	68
Part II Total	4,792	5,214	2,949
Simple assault	569	467	203
Larceny ($150)	1,532	1,840	1,056
Auto offense	435	591	313
Malicious mischief or arson	1,190	1,382	684
Counterfeiting or forgery	31	48	51
Fraud	217	334	220
Consumer fraud	135	133	110
Other sex	207	133	93
Family	331	191	118
Other victimization	145	95	101
Total	7,652	7,561	4,216
N	(9,661)	(10,491)	(11,837)

SOURCE: Philip H. Ennis, *Criminal Victimization in the United States: A Report of a National Survey* (Washington, D.C.: Government Printing Office, 1967), p. 24.

metropolis. In sum, the street is the arena of conflict and congruence which encapsulates the political, racial, and cultural experience of law and order.

The central city has been the sector within the metropolis most often subjected to close observation. The data in table 6-1 report the position of the central city relative to the other sectors of the metropolis. The general characteristics displayed there are not, by themselves, evidence of a crisis in the city, but they are the fundamental blocks on which current and impending problems of the central city are built. These data indicate that the central city has an overriding share of the least employable, poorest paid, least educated, and oldest and most fragile residents of the metropolis living beside a majority of less vulnerable suburbanites. This situation creates a highly complex set of service demands for the city administration.

In addition, the central city is the sector containing the largest number of racially diverse populations, which gives the city the appearance of a melting pot of social differences that is more myth than reality. Rather than living in a cooperative melting pot, the large city populations of blacks, Chicanos, Puerto Ricans, and whites live in a variety of segregated and partially segregated community patterns. The communities are often fraught with internal and cross-communal tensions which can erupt in socially disorderly and dislodging, or even violent, behaviors. The patterns of unemployment, tenements, black ghettos, barrios, old-age slums, and middle-class, working-class, and high-rise communities appear nonsystematic and disorderly.

Such social, cultural, and ethnic diversity describes a series of communities which defy easy service delivery solutions. The delivery of police service to the streets of this variegated sector of the metropolis is one of the most difficult chores for urban public servants and politicians. This irregular pattern of races, classes, and physically identifiable communities is the source of more criticism of and support for the police today than at any other time in the history of law enforcement in the United States. The responses of the police have been as uneven as the demands, criticism, and praise of the citizenry. The police are responding with increased imagination and innovation but at the same time are more stridently dissatisfied and formally and informally militant than ever before. The interaction between the police officer and the citizen has become a highly visible and vocal shouting match over a single public service, but the conflict represents the far more significant issues raised by the socially diverse nature of the cities' clientele and the frustrated attempts of the public sector to respond to highly differentiated and tension-filled demands.

Clientele:
Shades of Difference

In the context described above, the central city has become a focal point for the controversy over the most equitable and efficient administration of justice within the metropolis. The elusive concept of justice is a useful starting point for many social scientists because of the assumption that it is a desirable quality of a political system. Most scholars of police-community relations start with an assumption of justice maintenance similar to that put forth in a report of the President's Commission on Law Enforcement and Administration of Justice:

> The law enforcement officer plays a crucial role in the survival of our system of government by law, and in the maintenance of orderly social relations,

ideally expressed in the phrase *ordered liberty with justice.* Equal protection of the law is an extension of this principle, with its implication of respect for the rights of persons as persons.[14]

Most of the scholars mentioned earlier in the chapter who are concerned with discussing such a view of the police role use public perceptions as their mode of analysis and description. Without denying the utility of either the assumption of the President's Commission or of the study of attitudes, one scholar offers the following warning:

> Justice is difficult to measure. The justice of actions may be weighed by the perceptions of the actors. In this view, justice lies in the eye of the beholder. Justice depends on the expectation of the consumers, their perceptions of what treatment others receive, and the interpretation of their own experiences in terms of their personal values. Official actions contribute perceptions of justice and injustice but they do not determine them.[15]

Further, the variety of racial groups and classes representing the clientele of the various central cities of metropolitan areas makes categorization difficult. The behaviors of police and the perceptions and experiences of these diverse clientele differ from city to city. As a result, there is no accurate general treatment of the police function at the street level that applies uniformly to all urban places. General description is difficult, and accurate only at high levels of abstraction. However, the perceptions of and experiences with the police in different sectors of the city play an important part in the politics of policing. The attention directed at the increasing crime problem in this country and the allegations of an oppressive and unresponsive system of public service result from the perceptions and experiences people have with the servants of public order and the values they hold concerning "ordered liberty with justice" in society. Although such assessments of police by their clientele may be imprecise as applied to each street-level interaction between citizens and police, it remains important to explore them. They provide information about the sources of support and criticism of police among the city's diverse communities.

As discussed earlier, police scholar Michael Lipsky describes public criticism, at its most intense level, in warlike terms. For Lipsky, police

---

[14] The President's Commission on Law Enforcement and Administration of Justice, *Field Survey V: A National Survey of Police and Community Relations 1967* (Washington, D.C.: Government Printing Office, 1967), p. 6.

[15] Herbert Jacob, "Black and White Perceptions of Justice in the City," mimeographed (American Political Science Association Meeting, Los Angeles, California, September 8-12, 1970), p. 1.

officers, among other public servants, are "under siege. Their critics variously charge them with being insensitive, unprepared to work with ghetto residents, imcompetent, resistant to change and racist." [16] On the other hand, proponents of the police are just as adamant in their position that the police should be supported in this warlike atmosphere. The police are, in the eyes of this sector of the public, unfairly under siege—they are damned for what they do and damned for what they fail to do.[17] The sources of such criticisms and support rest in the values, perceptions, and experiences which accompany the social spread and diversity of differing metropolitan communities.

While the use of perceptions and expectations of city residents as measures of the effective outcome of police service is important, it has its shortcomings. Such measures assume that the distribution of justice services by the police officer is actually on the minds of city residents. To this end there is evidence, especially in core areas of cities, that this is at least a reasonable assumption. Albert Riess finds that:

> In many major metropolitan centers today, if not in the country as a whole, problems of crime and law enforcement command the attention of the public. For many inhabitants, particularly within the core of our cities, crime ranks first among the problems they regard as confronting our society.[18]

Coupled with this fear of crime, even with growing hostility, controversy, uncertainty, and emotional support swirling around the police officer in recent years, national studies by the National Opinion Research Center (NORC) indicate expanding populations holding high opinions of the police. NORC found that 67 percent of the population felt that the police were doing either an "excellent" or a "pretty good" job as compared to 54 percent in a similar study taken in 1963.[19] Studies also demonstrate that such support of the police is not exclusively found among whites. In a study of three core area precincts in Washington, D.C., one study found that "80 percent of the black males said that 'the police deserve more respect and thanks than they get.' " [20] However, to measure the outcome

---

[16] Michael Lipsky, "Street Level Bureaucracy and the Analysis of Urban Reform," *Urban Affairs Quarterly* (June 1971): 391.

[17] Klien, *The Police: Damned If they Do—Damned If They Don't.*

[18] Reiss, *Public Perceptions and Recollections.*

[19] The President's Commission on Law Enforcement and Administration of Justice, *Task Force Report: The Police* (Washington, D.C.: Government Printing Office, 1967), p. 145.

[20] Quoted by James Q. Wilson from a study by Albert D. Biderman et al. entitled *Report on a Pilot Study in the District of Columbia on Victimization and Attitudes Toward Law Enforcement* in "The Police in the Ghetto," in *The Police and the Community*, ed. Robert F. Steadman (Baltimore: The Johns Hopkins Press, 1972), pp. 53-54. In this article, Wilson reviews many of the national and local studies on positive assessments of police.

of police service by assessing people's perceptions and expectations of such services is relativistic. It assumes that, to the extent that such services are on the minds of the public, the police service *is* as people perceive it and *ought* to be as they expect it to be.[21]

The relativistic nature of perceptions of a public service is further convoluted by the fact that "perceptions are relative both to values held and to conditions around one." [22] Citizens in various communities within the metropolis incorporate their own and other's perceptions, values, and experiences into their personal assessment of the police service.

The result of such an absorption of collective judgments generated through living in a certain community or neighborhood helps explain differing levels of support and satisfaction with police service among different racially or class-defined communities. The experiences and values of the individuals of a city are always an evaluation of police service which is only partially objective. Each citizen's participation in the reflective evaluation that the relatively distinct community in which he resides places upon police service constitutes the remaining portion of his assessment of police service.

Finally, there is ambivalence within the United States over the proper role of police in a democratic society. Americans are hesitant to encourage any real or imagined dependency on a police force. Too much police power is perceived to be at odds with the functioning of democratic institutions. However, the quandry for the American city dweller deepens in the face of a deeply felt increase in violent crime. A recent study of neighborhoods in Boston and Chicago found that a majority (57 percent) of the populace think that there is "very much more" violent crime in their cities than in years past. The citizens are in

a kind of "double bind." They are skeptical, if not distrustful, of police power, yet they see police power as the most obvious solution to their problem. They respect the police function but are distrustful of them in some ways. They are sympathetic with them in the difficulty of their job, but seem afraid to allow them discretion. They fear the police but they fear crime more. . . .[23]

This general description of the clientele environment may seem a bit overdrawn; however, the following discussion of clientele attitudes toward the police function will bear out not only this ambivalence but also the

---

[21] Jacob, "Black and White Perceptions of Justice in the City," p. 1.

[22] Reiss, *Public Perceptions and Recollections*, p. 22.

[23] Ibid., p. 36.

cleavages between different racial and class groups within the city through their perceptions, expectations, and experiences with the police. And, while there are weaknesses in discussing the outcome of police service from this perspective, the dissonance experienced by citizens who find that their experiences or observations of the police do not measure up to their expectations, values, or perceptions of police is at the heart of the rising storm around police service.

Clientele and the Police:
A National Backdrop

While certain limited characteristics of national public opinion are applicable to public opinions about the police at the metropolitan level, for the most part there are very few universals which can be found to hold true for all communities within the central cities and other localities of the metropolis. Among the reasons for the lack of an authoritatively accurate typology of the public's attitudes toward police and police service are the following three. First, the relationship of police to the community and the image of the police which such a relationship engenders in the eyes of the public cannot be reasonably divorced from many of the larger issues of metropolitanism in general. Second, the relationships of police with their diverse clientele are different from city to city. Each city and metropolitan area has its own distinct blend of social groups, political personalities, and law enforcement issues. Third, the relationship of police and the community is often highly charged with emotion-laden rhetoric and allegations and counterallegations which distort the real satisfaction and dissatisfaction with the police.[24]

What there is of a general national image of the police is found scattered among the findings of various governmental studies, public opinion polls, and local studies.[25] The evidence from these sources may surprise those who have only read the attention-grabbing headlines which point to the growing dissatisfaction with the administration of the police function.

While a variety of particularly localized reasons exist for the lower levels of nonwhite satisfaction with police service, at the national level

---

[24] The President's Commission, *A National Survey of Police and Community Relations*, pp. 9-10.

[25] Various polls by Louis Harris, as well as G. D. Gourley, *Police and the Public* (Springfield, Ill.: C. C. Thomas, 1953); an October, 1965, survey conducted by WCBS-TV "Feedback" show, New York, New York; a citywide survey of San Diego, California, conducted by the San Diego city government in 1966. The last two studies are both cited in the President's Commission on Law Enforcement and Administration of Justice, *A National Survey of Police and Community Relations*, p. 12. Also, for a similar survey of Washington, D.C., residents see *Report of the President's Commission on Crime in the District of Columbia on the Metropolitan Police Department* (Washington, D.C.: Government Printing Office, 1966).

two basic complaints emerge from the studies of the President's Commission. Minority dissatisfaction with the police is generally voiced over (1) the "permissiveness" of law enforcement service and (2) a range of discriminatory behaviors practiced upon the minority poor by police. These complaints are described succinctly in a report of the U.S. Civil Rights Commission on "Police-Community Relations, Cleveland, Ohio":

> The complaints of the Negro community against the police department are legion. But the most frequent complaint is that of permissive law enforcement and that policemen fail to provide adequate protection and services in areas occupied by Negroes. There is also the complaint of police brutality, and closely associated with it is the allegation that police officers are discourteous to Negro residents and frequently subject them to verbal abuse. In addition, Negro residents complain about arrest and detention practices of the police department. They also vigorously criticize the way some demonstrators were arrested and the failure of the police to protect civil rights demonstrators from unlawful violence. Finally, Negroes argue that the police department practices discrimination in its personnel policies.[26]

Of the two complaints, the President's Commission found that the complaint of permissiveness was the most disturbing for ghetto residents. Black residents in particular view the alleged indifference of police to their requests for police service as tantamount to causing "criminal tyranny" in their neighborhoods. Such permissiveness is experienced in the perceived lack of involvement or concern of the police officer with the particular demands of ghetto residents, who often believe police service in the ghetto is slower, less professional, and more unsuccessful than service in white areas. It is felt that there is a particular tendency for the police to ignore crimes committed in the ghetto which would receive instant attention in white areas.

Second, there is a feeling that formal police techniques such as field interrogations and informal behaviors such as overt brutality and racially antagonistic language coalesce to deliver a discriminatory and oppressive service package to the ghetto resident.

However, ghetto residents represent only a minority of those living in the nation. Overall, most Americans feel that the police are doing a good to excellent job of law enforcement, as shown in table 6-4. From this table it is evident that in every sector of the nation a sizable majority of the population is quite satisfied with police service. Only in the cities does it appear that a substantial minority of the citizens are not very

---

[26] As quoted in the President's Commission, *A National Survey on Police and Community Relations*, p. 14.

satisfied. Further, the black population is just about split in its evaluation of the success of the law enforcement institutions at the local level. It is also interesting to see that as the law enforcement force (federal and state) becomes more removed from the citizen and less visible, the citizen is more apt to rate the job such an agency does higher.

TABLE 6-4

Ratings of Law Enforcement
("How would you rate the job the federal (state, local) government does on law enforcement—excellent, pretty good, only fair, or poor? ")

	Good-Excellent		Rating
	Federal %	State %	Local %
Nationwide	76	70	65
By size of place			
Cities	80	67	57
Suburbs	79	71	72
Towns	75	72	65
Rural	71	72	66
By race			
White	75	71	67
Black	81	63	51

Source: A Louis Harris Poll used by the President's Commission on Law Enforcement and Administration of Justice, *A National Survey of Police and community Relations, 1967*, p. 10.

A follow-up survey of the President's Commission discovered that the nation's white population was more satisfied with the departments actually serving it compared to other departments than was the nation's black population (see table 6-5). These findings bear out the general patterns of dissatisfaction of black citizens discussed previously. The Commission attributes the lack of support for the police among the minority of the white population to the attitudes of "the lower socio-economic groups who have the same general complaints against the police as the minority groups and some whites who are, for want of a better name, of a 'liberal bent.' " [27] Although the vast majority of the white population appear to support the police, the Commission adds that perhaps "support" is too strong a word in every case. It found a good amount of apathy toward law enforcement. For many among the white majority who support the police the Commission said

---

[27] Ibid., p. 20.

they seldom see the police as perfect, but do visualize steady improvement and are willing to wait for slow and steady change. Their feelings seem to be that as we improve police salaries we will get better men and in the meantime the police are doing a pretty good job under difficult conditions.[28]

TABLE 6-5

Relative Rating of Local Police Departments
("On the basis of your knowledge of American police departments, how does your police department compare with others? ")

	Excellent %	Above Average %	Average %	Below Average %	Poor %
White	20	50	25	5	0
Black	2	26	43	23	6

SOURCE: President's Commission on Law Enforcement and Administration of Justice, *Field Survey V: A National Survey of Police and Community Relations, 1967* (Washington, D.C.: Government Printing Office, 1967), p. 11.

These overall patterns of public opinion are part of a report of the President's Commission which concludes that to the extent that there is a fundamental national public opinion about police,

the picture is one of general support for the police as they are now performing their duties from the majority of the population. However, a small minority of the white population and near majorities of the Negro population are deeply disturbed by present police practices and philosophy.[29]

The police view with equal disdain and dismay the strident demands and foreign conditions of minorities on the one hand and the apathy and lack of real support of the dominant white community on the other. "They are dismayed by the fact that they are compelled to 'save' a public that does not want to be 'saved' . . . . There is a strong feeling of frustration among police that they have been abandoned in the war against crimes." [30]

At the same time they view as unfair both the criticisms and special demands for service which are most present in the ghettos of the minority

---

[28] Ibid.

[29] Ibid., p. 13.

[30] Ibid., p. 21.

poor. They argue that most claims of unequal service and police brutality are unwarranted and many of the demands for service should be made to social workers, housing inspectors, or marriage counselors, but not to them.

Three Central Cities and
Attitudes toward Police

Beyond this rather general reading of national attitudes of clientele and police, any universally applicable statement about the police function would be impossible. Therefore, a detailed assessment of the diverse clientele and their attitudes toward the police will, of necessity, need to be obtained from experiences in select communities. Three such central cities have been selected to display the more particular local environment of opinions and attitudes which are directed toward police: Denver, Colorado; Rochester, New York; and Milwaukee, Wisconsin. These three communities were the subjects of three studies conducted at about the same time in the latter part of the 1960s. They represent three of the more comprehensive studies conducted on clientele assessments of the police function and are analyses of more representative and less dramatic metropolitan communities than the volatile centers of New York, Los Angeles, Detroit, and Newark, whose experiences took such a large share of the headlines of the recent past.

In their study of Denver, Bayley and Mendelsohn measured the perceptions of the black and Spanish-speaking communities toward the police. This study was selected to offer information concerning primarily minority perceptions, expectations, and experiences.[31]

In the study of Rochester, Perry was concerned with measuring the image of the police function in the black community of Rochester, as well as finding out just how far removed this image was from that of dominant white residents of the same community who were served by similar street-level policemen. Hence this study is used primarily as a resource for a discussion of racial diversity and cleavage within the central city. It is concerned with placing alleged minority criticisms of the police in the context of criticisms or support found in the dominant white community.[32]

[31] David H. Bayley and Harold Mendelsohn, *Minorities and the Police: Confrontation in America* (New York: The Free Press, 1969).

[32] David C. Perry, "Police Service in a Dual Society: A Study of the Urban Context of Police Service and its Problems in the City of Rochester, New York " (Ph.D. dissertation, Syracuse University, 1971). See also David C. Perry and Paula A. Sornoff, *Politics at the Street Level: The Select Case of Police Administration and the Community* (Beverly Hills, Calif.: Sage Publications, 1973).

In his study of Milwaukee, Herbert Jacob extended the study of various clientele groups to include class differentials as well as racial cleavages. He studied three small distinct neighborhoods within Milwaukee. The first neighborhood was a black ghetto community, the second a predominantly white working-class neighborhood, and the last a middle-class white community at the fringe of the city.[33]

In each of these studies, the distinct intracentral city communities were distinguished by differing socioeconomic characteristics similar to ones used previously in this chapter. Such socioeconomic designations within the highly populated and more densely confined central city jurisdictions make their relatively high levels of heterogeneity an important characteristic against which to measure differing perceptions of the police function. The studies taken collectively are not meant to represent a comprehensive view of clientele attitudes regarding the street-level activities of the police, but they do act as an interesting collage of the types of attitudinal and emotional dynamics which permeate the environment of the street as the police officer goes about his day-to-day activities. Further, the attitudes of these sectors of the selected communities indicate some of the sensitive factors which pervade a special part of local government service delivery—the politics of the street.

The conflict between perceptions, values, and experiences; the ambivalence over the role of such public servants as the police; and the tension of racial and class proximity which pervade the life of those living in the city are integral parts of the provision of most local services today. These are parts of public policy functions which are not adequately recognized by studying simply the fiscal jurisdictional or structural components of service delivery.

The remainder of this section will treat four areas of community identity within central cities which attend social spread and diversity. First, the general outlook on life shared by residents of racially differentiated communities within the central city will be discussed. Such an approach should help to identify and understand the environment of the street in which police officers operate. Second, this section will be concerned with the importance that people in different communities within the central city attach to the adequacy of police service, and the extent to which the police service they presently receive is a problem for them. Such considerations by the citizens will be discussed within the context of how they rank or compare such law enforcement issues with other problems they face while living in the metropolis. This approach should shed light on the importance of police service to citizens of differing racial and class identities.

---

[33] Jacob, "Black and White Perceptions of Justice in the City."

Third, the images of the police as individuals and as public servants in the minds of clientele groups from various socioeconomic sectors of the city will be examined. This section will also discuss the readiness of the citizens to support the local police. Fourth, the experiences or contacts which clientele have with the police and the extent to which this affects their perceptions of the police and the quality of the service they provide will be considered. The patterns of clientele attitudes in these four areas vary in the three cities under consideration; however, the evidence suggests general intracity patterns of agreement.

This section uses the attitudes of clientele within communities distinguished by the characteristics of race, income, and employment. However, to succumb to generalizations about blacks or middle-class whites in universal terms from the finding that a high percentage of a group feels one way or another is to fall prey to what social scientists call the "ecological fallacy." [34] While a certain attitude may be identified as prevalent in a majority of homes of the community, it is by no means a universal view held by all residents. The following discussion will use the general racial and class terms to identify communities and discuss the attitudes of these communities. It should be understood, however, that no inference of universality of attitudes is applied to any population group, unless specified.

A further consideration is in order at this point. It does not necessarily follow that because a certain group of blacks, whites, or police hold certain attitudes, they will behave in ways which are always consistent with their attitudes. To neglect this condition is to neglect

> The important ways in which society intervenes between beliefs and actions by creating a range of expectations, roles, rewards, sanctions, and constraints that powerfully influence behavior and modify the motivating power of attitudes.[35]

Attitudes are used in the study of police-community relations because they help us to understand the environment of tension and acceptance which can directly or indirectly make the police officer's job more or less difficult. In short, they are one of the best avenues to better understanding police at the street level.

Environment. In the central city are found different publics exhibiting a wide range of diverse social and economic characteristics which combine

---

[34] Ibid., pp. 1-9.
[35] Wilson, "The Police in the Ghetto," p. 65.

to create a service environment composed of life styles and world views. The clientele with such differing experiences and views of life are often quite foreign and even antagonistic to each other. These differences, by themselves, are enough to make the role of the police officer at the street level hard to define. Rochester is a good example of a city composed of such differing clientele groups. In the study of police in Rochester, two representative communities were isolated and identified *within the city.* "Representative" signified that community within the inner city (IC) or outside inner city (OIC) which was most reflective of it in terms of race, income, age, education, family composition, and housing conditions. Therefore, the communities which were studied were, like the metropolitan area of Rochester itself, *not* dramatic extremes of racial and class differences but rather representative of relatively average central city neighborhoods in a relatively average metropolitan area. Both of these communities were served by city police officers working out of the same station house, who often worked both districts.

The IC community of Rochester is 75 percent nonwhite (all but a small portion of whom are black), 5 percent Irish and 4.4 percent German. It has a median age of 28.5 years and median education level of 11.7 years, the housing is predominantly rental, and the median family income is $6,860. The characteristics of income, education, and age of blacks approximate similar characteristics found in the general socioeconomic profile of metropolitanism discussed previously. The OIC community is totally white and is 32 percent Irish and 26 percent German. Its median age is 48 years, and its level of educational achievement is 12.4. The predominant housing characteristic is home ownership, and the median income is $9,000.

The neighborhoods are, therefore, distinct. The IC community is economically poorer and significantly younger than the white neighborhood. The IC residents are slightly less educated and do not have the type of economic stake in the neighborhood that attends home ownership. While we can, for all practical purposes, call the IC neighborhood "black," there remain certain "white" pockets which allow the community to retain a tinge of transition. The OIC community is still very white. Its largest subpopulations are ethnics of German or Irish stock, although most of these persons are now second and third generation. On the surface such information would predict different lifestyles for the two communities. Indications of such lifestyle differences can be found in the ways in which the respective residents view their environment, the other community, and the outside world in general.

In response to a question about how they felt "about some things concerning life in general," the differences in these central city communities became apparent. The question included a set of descriptions of "life in general" designed to discover the residents' conceptions of their life in the city and how positively or negatively they perceived their present patterns of living. More than 50 percent of IC dwellers agreed with the assertion that life for the IC dweller is "getting worse rather than better"; "there are few persons you can count on"; and therefore, "all you can do is live life one day at a time." "With very little to look forward to," it seems "hardly fair to bring children into the world." As a result of such views, better than 50 percent of the IC dwellers have "little trust in local government and politicians" and have a strong feeling that "the police are not about to provide the IC dweller with the same type of service they provide others in the city."

The OIC dwellers disagreed with this assessment of life in general at almost exactly the same levels (more than 50% disagree "strongly" or "slightly") of intensity that the IC dwellers voiced in their agreement with this outlook on life. Life for the residents of the white OIC was much more fruitful, full of hope, and meaningful for themselves and for their children.

In the area of politics and the threat of rising crime, the populace of both communities seemed to indicate rather substantial agreement. Both felt that neither their property nor their personal safety on the street was necessarily secure from illegal attack or trespass. Both groups also felt that there was little use carrying their individual complaints to their political leaders "because often they (politicians) aren't really interested in the problems of the average man." However, even here, the IC residents demonstrated a much stronger conception of their plight than did the OIC residents. Responding to the statement "One's property (car, house, etc.) isn't safe anymore, we have to lock everything all the time," 78.8 percent of the OIC residents and 91.0 percent of the IC residents agreed. At the same time, 77.4 percent of the IC and 75.4 percent of the OIC residents believe that "a person can't walk down his own street and feel safe." Finally, while 52.5 percent of the OIC residents believe local politicians to be unresponsive to their needs, 74.5 percent of the IC residents concur.[36]

The IC community's dissatisfaction with its environment is more than matched by its restive posture concerning the extent to which its rights and complaints are being ignored. Of the IC populace, 68.6 percent believe that the minority/poor of the city are "not pressing hard enough" in expressing their dissatisfaction over their civil rights and other complaints. Of the OIC, 54.4 percent believe that the minority/poor of the city are

---

[36] Perry, "Police Service in a Dual Society." p. 124.

"pressing too hard" and 17.5 percent of the OIC residents feel that the minority/poor "should not be pressing at all." At the same time, only 10.5 percent of the OIC respondents believe that overall there is "quite a bit of bad treatment of the Negro and Spanish-speaking groups by police in Rochester," while 53.2 percent of the IC population believe this to be true assessment of the present situation in the city.

These findings seem to indicate that there are significantly strong feelings reflecting the positive and satisfactory environment of the OIC. The IC is not only displeased with its general environment, but it is also dissatisfied with the present level of pressure its representatives are placing on those in power to provide more satisfactory conditions—the pressure, in the mind of the IC clientele, should be increased.

Thus far only general questions relating to the service of law enforcement have been discussed, but it is readily evident that problems of law and order are important to residents of both the inner city and the outside inner city. The "negative" and "alienated" conception of life in the inner city is made especially clear when juxtaposed to the more satisfied responses of the OIC clientele. Not only does the OIC seem relatively satisfied with its own environment, but it also appears to be annoyed with residents who raise complaints about their own environments.

The Relative Importance of Police Service.   There can be little doubt that fear of crime is a primary concern of many living in metropolitan areas today. In 1968, a Gallup poll found that crime had displaced other concerns as the most serious domestic problem. Reiss's studies of high crime areas in Boston and Chicago for the President's Commission on Law Enforcement and Administration of Justice display patterns of urgent paranoia among the residents of these two cities. The studies revealed that anywhere from 35 percent to 43 percent of core area residents stay off the streets and do not speak to strangers. When they have to travel the streets at night, they go by car or cab. As a result, one-fifth of those interviewed would like to move to another neighborhood.[37] The white and black communities of Rochester agreed that they were afraid when walking the streets of their own neighborhoods, and they felt it necessary to lock things at all times.

The fear of crime notwithstanding, the communities discussed here are not as concerned with police service and crime as they are with some other problems in their urban environment. In Denver, when asked to list the problems in the city which they found "the most hard to bear," black and Spanish-speaking minorities listed discrimination and prejudice

---

[37] Reiss, *Public Perceptions and Recollections,* pp. 102-3.

as primary, followed by inadequate employment opportunities. Problems of police service were ranked fourth by blacks and sixth by Spanish-heritage residents.

Attempting to further break down the ways in which different groups perceived police service, the authors of the Denver study asked the residents of the white, black, and Spanish-heritage communities to list the particular problems which face poor people in Denver. All groups agreed that the prime problem was that of "making ends meet." Following the problem of preserving the household pocketbook were problems of education, housing, and employment. Police "harassment" and "brutality" ranked highly among only the black and Spanish-heritage communities (and here it was listed eighth behind the more basic concerns of economic and physical problems).

Asked to name one thing they would most like to see improved in the city, the minority communities were more apt to name physical improvements such as recreational facilities, sewers, street lights, and housing repairs than improvements in police protection.[38] While there is a growing preoccupation nationally with the problems of crime and a particular concern with racial discrimination and eduation, the minority residents of Denver seem to be rather pragmatic—specifying traditionally incremental physical improvements in their neighborhoods rather than the larger issues of rising crime or safety in the streets. The paradox of citizen concern with inadequate police service and rising crime, yet apparent lack of interest in the issue when asked to specify primary changes in the climate of the city, seems to reflect the historical ambivalence of the American people toward the police function and the heightened cynicism in general toward various public institutions and their ability to solve the problems of contemporary metropolitanism.[39]

The perceptions of police service as a problem in Rochester follow approximately the same patterns found in Denver. In Rochester, however, police service and behavior are more significant problems in black neighborhoods (IC) than in the dominant white neighborhoods (OIC) of the city. While the IC was primarily concerned with changes or improvements in race relations and civil rights, the OIC was most concerned with changes and improvements in the physical environment of the city. It is interesting to note that the physical environment ranked next to last on the IC's list of priorities and race relations was ranked next to last by residents of the OIC. Changes or improvements in public safety were the prime consideration for 14.6 percent of the IC population and 5.2 percent of

---

[38] Bayley and Mendelsohn, *Minorities and the Police*, pp. 138-40.

[39] See chapter 4, p. 85.

the OIC population, ranking fourth and next to last, respectively, among the list of nine issues identified by each sample.

These findings show that although crime may be a problem for members of all communities within the central city, it does not appear to be the problem in most serious need of attention as defined by the residents. It appears that a resident responds strongly only when directly asked whether crime and the attendant police response is a problem. Left alone to rank the problems as he sees them, he is not likely to rank problems of public safety highly. The residents of Rochester seem to offer attitudinal patterns which have a relatively contemporary ring to them. Blacks are most concerned with problems of racial oppression and whites are most concerned with issues of environmental protection. Both groups are put off by politicians and, to a varying extent, by public servants such as police. Finally, racially different communities seem to have little respect for the issues considered important by the other community. In fact whites consider the problems of race to be overstated and not worthy of the political pressures which blacks consider to be vital. As a result, the police officer is faced with serving communities that may be in close proximity but are basically estranged from each other and have different concerns. The police officer is almost an ambassador who must learn to serve and order communities who remain foreign to each other.

Public Images of the Police. Perhaps no other public servant conjures up as many stereotypes, fantasies, and criticisms as the patrolman. He is a "pig" to some and a "white knight" to others. He must carry out his responsibilities in an environment made more hostile by these caricatures. Often these fantasies become a source of confrontation and an eventual situation of disorder.

Whatever caricatures people draw of the patrolman, there seems to be a generally high regard for the role of policemen in society. In both Denver and Rochester, better than 69 percent of all those interviewed say that the policeman's job is either "much more important" or "somewhat more important" than other jobs. Being important, however, does not necessarily mean that the residents of these diverse communities within the central cities of Denver and Rochester were in agreement as to the amount of respect or prestige to attach to present occupants of the job or to the job itself. What this does mean is that most members of the central city, regardless of race or class, see the job of patrolman as an important role to be maintained in urban society.[40]

---

[40] Bayley and Mendelsohn, *Minorities and the Police*, pp. 36-38; Perry, "Police Service in a Dual Society," p. 136.

Although the black community of Rochester sees great efficacy in the role of policemen, it does not appear to be extremely supportive of the type of service they are getting from the present police force. While 74.4 percent of the IC residents conceive of the job as "more" or "somewhat more important" than other jobs, only 24.8 percent are willing to vote for an increase in the present police officers' salaries.

Perhaps the IC's reticence to increase the salary of a group of public servants which they conceive of as providing a vital service to society is based on their concern that more taxes will deplete already comparatively low family incomes. However, it appears that this issue cuts more deeply. As one respondent suggested:

> We would have to be crazy to want to pay more to people to serve us less. By less I mean it would be masochistic to pay a guy even more to treat you with a disrespect that tells you he thinks you're less than human. I'm not saying that police aren't important, and I'm willing to pay for the good service, but I won't pay more for what I'm getting in misservice [sic] now." [41]

White residents of Rochester register strong support for a tax raise for police salaries with 64.9 percent answering in the affirmative when asked this question. White residents in Rochester appear to be more satisfied with the *type* of patrolman who services them. This view is not dissimilar from that held by white residents in the white working-class and white middle-class neighborhoods of Milwaukee (see table 6-6). Jacob asked residents of these communities what police officers *actually* were, then supplied the set of opposite adjectives found in table 6-6. The residents then scored their perceptions of police along the adjectival scales from one to seven. Table 6-6 reports the means of these scores for each class neighborhood. Jacob found that:

> Blacks perceive the police as more corrupt, more unfair, more excitable, more harsh, tougher, weaker, lazier, less intelligent, less friendly, more cruel, and more on the bad than good side than white respondents in either of the two other neighborhoods. Whites, while not in perfect agreement with one another, were closer to each other than to the black ghetto respondents. Middle-class whites generally gave more favorable ratings to the police than whites in the working class neighborhood. But the differences are smaller than those between either set of white respondents and the blacks. [42]

The attitudes and perceptions of the police described thus far detail a series of highly diverse conceptions of the police function which show

---

[41] Perry, "Police Service in a Dual Society," p. 137.

[42] Jacob, "Black and White Perceptions of Justice in the City," p. 3.

TABLE 6-6

Perceptions of Police in Three Neighborhoods
in Milwaukee

Scales (1—Score—7)	Ghetto (N=71)	White Working Class (N=71)	White Middle Class (N=73)	F Ratio	P
Honest—Corrupt	3.30	2.25	1.84	13.10	.001
Bad—Good	4.10	6.04	6.10	35.78	.001
Unfair—Fair	3.76	5.65	6.03	27.70	.001
Excitable—Calm	3.42	5.69	4.97	22.37	.001
Lazy—Hardworking	4.62	5.86	5.85	10.60	.001
Smart—Dumb	2.76	1.93	2.03	6.39	.002
Friendly—Unfriendly	3.63	2.06	2.08	17.38	.001
Kind—Cruel	3.82	2.14	2.10	22.34	.001
Strong—Weak	2.66	2.04	2.12	3.09	.048
Harsh—Easygoing	3.04	3.86	3.68	3.30	.039
Tough—Softhearted	2.49	3.24	2.70	3.24	.041

SOURCE: Herbert Jacob, "Black and White Perceptions of Justice in the City, " mimeographed (American Political Science Association meeting, Los Angeles, California, September 8-12, 1970), p. 3.

varying levels of acceptance of the police in different neighborhoods. These perceptual differences are but a part of the picture. Although the data indicate strongly identified differences in the images and perceptions of the police function, there are sizable numbers of persons in each of the racially or class differentiated neighborhoods who do not hold such perceptions.

> Consequently, there is substantial overlap between the samples [taken in different neighborhoods]. Some blacks have perceptions that are more favorable to the police than that of some whites. One cannot predict on the basis of race alone how favorable or unfavorable a person's perceptions of the police will be.[43]

Police-Clientele Contact. The nature of police contact with the citizen is not only influenced by the extent the police officer is fulfilling an important function, but also by the extent to which the citizen feels that the police officer is a public servant worthy of respect. The black community of Rochester is more convinced that the police officers of the city treat members of the minority/poor community "often unfairly" or in a "definitely prejudiced" manner (40.1 percent) than the OIC or white community, 61.4 percent of which feels that minority/poor residents of

---

[43] Ibid., p. 4.

the IC are "usually treated fairly." [44] General images of individual treatment of the police when citizen-police contact is made and the distinct
environments in which police operate are most dramatically displayed
by attitudes toward the police over the issue of police brutality.

In Rochester, 40 percent of the OIC sample population do not feel
that police brutality exists at all, while only 3 percent of the minority/poor
inner city support this view. Seventy-five percent of the dominant white
OIC neighborhood believe that charges of police brutality, harrassment,
or mistreatment of minorities are "mostly false," while 60 percent of the
minority/poor population of the IC feel that these charges are "mostly"
or "sometimes" true. Such a divergence of opinion can be related to degree
of contact with the police. Only 7 percent of the OIC group have ever
observed or experienced personally such treatment, while about 30 percent
of the IC neighborhood group state they have observed or experienced
such treatment.

The National Advisory Commission on Civil Disorders reports similar
findings in a study of 6,000 persons in fifteen cities (see table 6-7). Blacks
were more critical of the police on all characterizations of police brutality
across all age levels. Here again, actual experience with brutality partially
influenced opinions. Age, as well as race and contact, were also factors
fueling a high level of criticism of the police.

White communities are getting increasingly older in the central cities
of this nation and black communities are younger. Hence, the age of black
ghettos, the racial history and conditions of the neighborhood environment,
and the overall negative outlook on many aspects of life which permeates
many inner city minority/poor communities combine to set forth a harsh
and highly critical view of the police officer as one who controls a sup-
pressed environment and stands for many. The white communities, less
discouraged and more supportive of the police in general, find charges
of police brutality distinctly less credible.

Perhaps the credibility of the actual charges of police brutality is not
the central issue. Even if the charges of police brutality are untrue, the
very fact that people think them to be true is significant. The cry of
"brutality" may well symbolize other issues which form the slum. The
police officer can be easily identified as the representative of a system
which caused these conditions and becomes the target for criticism and
attack.

Beyond the issue of allegedly brutal contact with police are the more
traditional contacts one has with the police: calls for help, arrests, traffic
violations, or auto accidents. In the Rochester study, the OIC sample
reported a much higher contact rate with the police than the IC: 52.6

---

[44] Perry, "Police Service in a Dual Society," pp. 152-53.

TABLE 6-7

Attitudes toward the Police
(Based on a Survey of 6,000 Persons in Fifteen Cities)

Age Group	Believe It Has Happened		Happened to Them	
(both sexes)	White	Black	White	Black
	a. "Police Use Insulting Language"			
16-19	24%	55%	14%	24%
20-29	24	45	11	19
30-39	14	37	7	14
40-49	13	36	3	15
50-59	9	26	6	7
60-69	8	24	3	5
	b. "Police Frisk and Search Without Good Reason"			
16-19	25%	51%	12%	22%
20-29	15	43	5	18
30-39	7	33	2	11
40-49	9	32	2	9
50-59	7	28	1	4
60-69	4	24	1	8
	c. "Police Rough People Up Unnecessarily"			
16-19	25%	49%	3%	8%
20-29	13	43	1	7
30-39	7	33	3	3
40-49	5	30	0	2
50-59	6	26	1	4
60-69	3	20	0	1

SOURCE: Angus Campbell and Howard Schuman, "Racial Attitudes in Fifteen American Cities," in *Supplemental Studies for the National Advisory Commission on Civil Disorders* (Washington, D.C.: Government Printing Office, 1968), p. 44.

percent of the OIC had called the police at least once, while only 37.2 percent of the IC stated that they had called the police. In Milwaukee, similar patterns were in evidence. Blacks reported more contact with the police in calls for help and arrests, and whites report more contact with the police in traffic violations and auto accidents. The black population of Milwaukee was decidedly less satisfied with police service during such contacts than the whites of working-class or middle-class neighborhoods. Such dissatisfaction could stem from the type of service the police officer was administering—the contacts with the white residents were, on the whole, less tension-laden and less dramatic than those in the black ghetto. From table 6-8 it is evident that, in Rochester, a similar pattern exists. There is a difference in the types of calls for help from the OIC and IC areas:

The most prevalent call for service in the OIC concerned complaints over "noise" from speeding cars and children. In all, these calls make up 44.0 percent of all OIC calls, while another 20 percent are "low risk" calls—i.e.,

TABLE 6-8

Reasons for Calling a Patrolman

	IC			OIC	
	n	%		n	%
Prowler	3	8.3	House Break-in	6	24.0
Robbery	9	25.0	Disturbing Peace		
			(Autos, kids, noise)	11	44.0
Auto Accident	3	8.3	Vandals	1	4.0
Disturbing Peace (Kids)	5	13.8	Watch House (On		
Assault	1	2.8	Vacation)	2	8.0
Family Fight	8	22.8	Assault	1	4.0
Child Lost	2	5.5	Stolen Bicycles,		
Auto Violation	2	5.5	Hub Caps	2	8.0
Racial Fight	2	5.5	Argument	1	4.0
Illness	1	2.8	Auto Accidents	1	4.0
Totals	36	99.7%		25	100.0%

Source: David C. Perry and Paula A. Sornoff, *Politics at the Street Level: The Select Case of Police Administration and the Community* (Beverly Hills, Calif.: Sage Publications, 1973), p. 20.

involving a low degree of violence in either securing an arrest or undertaking an order maintenance request. Low-risk calls might involve a stolen bicycle or request to watch a house during the owner's vacation, or an auto accident. Thus, in the OIC, a full 64 percent of the demands for police service do not contain an ostensible potential for "violence." Conversely, only 34.1 percent of the calls for police service in the IC are "low risk" by nature: illness, auto accident, child lost, auto violation and the like. These account for 22.1 percent of the overall demand for police service, while "disturbing the peace" accounts for only 13.8 percent of all IC calls for police service.

When it comes to potentially "violent" or "high risk" incidents which require police service (prowler, robbery, family fights, and racial fights), 64.9 percent of the IC respondents discussed such incidents as compared to 36 percent of the OIC residents. The evident "high risk" nature of service demands in the IC as compared to the OIC demonstrates a need for a different type of police service. These data also indicate the existence of a potentially higher degree of tension between the police, the victim, and the offender in calls in the IC area other than with calls from the OIC area.[45]

Such tension-filled contacts in the IC with high levels of risk for both the citizen and police officer and low returns in terms of service satisfaction (i.e., potential solution of a crime, arrest of one or more parties involved, or a dramatic and unsettling experience) coalesce to increase the probability of dissatisfaction with the behavior and service of the police officer.

[45] This excerpt from *Politics at the Street Level: The Select Case of Police Administration and the Community*, by David C. Perry and Paula A. Sornoff is reprinted from *Sage Professional Paper in Administrative and Policy Studies* vol. 1, no. 03-008 (1973), pp. 19-20 by permission of the publisher, Sage Publications, Inc.

Police on the Street

The heart of the police function is found in the activities of the patrolman on the street. The police officer is, in a real sense, a "man in the middle"— an agent of a government employed, in part, to manage the "dirty work" of society. As such, the beat patrolman becomes the target of criticism for those citizens of the metropolis who have suffered the most from the failures of the governments and economic institutions to provide an environment of economic opportunity and social and racial acceptance. Further, the complex attitudes which descend upon the police officer and the duties of his job place him in a position of social isolation relative to his fellow citizens. Such isolation works against a healthy or uniformly strong self-image for the officer and his role. Such conditions often create and reinforce service behaviors which are at best uneven and at worst actions of malfeasance, racism, or illegality. Though he is not merely buffeted by forces exclusively outside his control, the experiences of the police officer on today's metropolitan street is a study, at times, of the overarching confusion and unmet needs of metropolitanism in general and not simply a study of the successes and failures of the police function in particular. He is playing a role over which he has only partial control— he is, in a way, a victim of his central position in a great number of the cross-cutting pressures of living as well as servicing the metropolis. Such "victimization" is manifest in a variety of ways.

First, in his relations with the diverse communities of the city and the metropolis, the patrolman finds himself the target of competing pressures which do little to ease the burdens of his role. Such relations with the public take him to "the heart of such questions as civil rights and crime, and at least tangentially . . . to the problems of urbanization and poverty." [46] As an agent of the state he is embroiled in concerns of the state and the socially disparate concerns of the public, many of which he is neither sworn to uphold nor professionally capable of dealing with. Hence he becomes a respresentative of the weaknesses of the public service delivery system of the state and, in a sense, a victim of the larger patterns of sociopolitical confusion of the metropolis. Joseph Gusfield points out that such

> agents of government are the only persons in modern society who can legitimately claim to represent the total society. . . . This representational

[46] The President's Commission on Law Enforcement and Administration of Justice, *A National Survey of Police and Community Relations*, p. 9.

character of government officials and their acts makes it possible for them not only to influence the allocation of resources, but also to define the public norms of morality and to designate which acts violate them.[47]

Given the image of representative of the political system of the country and the ability or at least the opportunity to apply his own style to such representation, the police officer is placed in an extremely important yet highly tenuous position, particularly in today's urban ghettos. Many minority/poor residents see much that is wrong with the way the political process works for them. The system is viewed as oppressive and racist and the ghetto stands as *de facto* evidence that their community has not received its share of political and economic resources. By their very position in the lower class, ghetto residents demand special services which respond directly to their vulnerable position and would, if provided, allow them greater access to the social and economic opportunities available to the upper- and middle-class communities of the metropolis. Police who do not respond to such selective needs will be viewed by some as representative of a society which is unresponsive and as agents who join in the suppression of the class and racial grievances of the ghetto. Hence the police officer becomes a "victim" of social pressures and issues which are neither of his making nor within his professional scope. The President's Commission puts this problem of policing more particularly:

> [T]he police are victims of community problems which are not of their making. For generations, minority groups and the poor have not received a fair opportunity to share the benefits of American life. They suffer from bad housing, inferior education, unemployment, underemployment, or low wages. They have been discriminated against and abused by welfare and public housing officials, private landlords and businessmen. Their frustrations and bitterness are taken out, at least in part, on the policeman as the most visible symbol of a society and its law which have often treated them so unjustly.[48]

The social and economic disparities and diversities discussed in the first section of this chapter take on a dual meaning in this context. First, they describe the basic social conditions of the metropolis which confront the police officer. Second, the disparities identify communities or subsections

---

[47] Joseph R. Gusfield, "Moral Passage: The Symbolic Process of Public Designations of Deviance," in *Law and the Behavioral Sciences*, ed. L. Friedman and S. Macauley, p. 308 (Indianapolis, Ind.: Bobbs–Merrill, 1969).

[48] The President's Commission on Law Enforcement and the Administration of Justice, *Task Force Report: The Police* (Washington, D.C.: Government Printing Office, 1967), p. 150.

within the city and metropolis with different needs, expectations and aspirations.

The police officer is also, in part, a victim of the formal and, often unrealistic, definition of his particular role. This condition is evidenced by the code to which a recruit is introduced when he enters the police force:

> His duty is to be an enforcement officer, an unbiased fact-finding agent of the law, and not an executioner. He should leave the conclusions and the verdicts to the judiciary. . . . The officer must be flexible in the enforcement of the laws of the land, not in applying all laws differently to different people but in the process of applying all the laws to all the people. . . . The educated wealthy and the gang from across the tracks must be met and dealt with on the level of their understanding, all within the law.

> Part of the glamour and respectability that surrounds an officer, if such be the case, is based on his clean ruggedness. He is expected to be fearless, firm and unaffected by the emotions which furnish the drive for most people. Making an arrest is an ungentle business at its best and a brutal business at its worst.[49]

The police officer, from the day he enters the training academy and reads a statement similar to this one, is told that he is an agent of formal legal equality who must apply all the laws equally without regard for the position of people or their plight outside the particular law they may have broken. In short, as James Wilson puts it,

> formally the police are supposed to have almost no discretion: by law in many places and in theory everywhere they are supposed to arrest everyone they see committing an offense, or with regard to more serious offenses, everyone they have reasonable cause to believe has committed an offense.[50]

Such a philosophy of professionalism leads to cries of insensitivity from some citizens and feelings of acute frustration for the police officer. He is supposed to uphold in theory every law—tens of thousands of them—and he must do it with impartiality and antiseptic objectivity. The police officer finds, in reality, this is quite impossible.

First, he cannot know all the laws he must enforce. Such an overload of legislation and rule making leads to arbitrary and frustrating conditions which subvert the alleged even-handedness of the patrolman's function.

---

[49] Rochester Municipal Training Council, "The Law in His Hands" (Rochester, N.Y.: Basic Training Council Supplementary Materials, n.d.).

[50] Wilson, *Varieties of Police Behavior*, p. 7.

He may be guided by certain administrative or political special interests to enforce some laws and forget to enforce others. Police specialist Dan Dodsen, in alluding to the great number of laws which delineate citizen behaviors as illegal, points out that:

> No policeman enforces all the laws of a community. If he did, we would all be in jail before the end of the first day. The laws which are selected for enforcement are those which the power structure of the community wants enforced. The police official's job is dependent upon his having radar-like equipment to sense what is the power structure and what it wants enforced as laws.[51]

The police officer resents this need to maintain a "radar-like" sense of what the politicians and administrators want of him more than any other single aspect of his job. The police interviewed in Rochester listed their basic "headache or problem of being a police officer" as "interference of politicians in the police bureau and in the courts." This type of interference included political influence from city hall, liberal "do-gooders" who favored lenient sentencing, and liberal "do-nothing" judges. The basic recommendation for change suggested by police officers in Rochester, therefore, was not at all surprising—"get the judges and politicians out of our jobs and off our backs."

The result of such alleged meddling on the part of politicians and judges in their lives has had an effect on the Rochester police bureau which is found all over the country—a significant lowering in police morale. Again, the main reasons cited by better than half of the police officers for "low" or "very low" morale among the members of the bureau are:

> (1) the interference of politicians into the role of the police department in the community, (2) the perceived leniency of the courts, and (3) the basic work conditions of the department (in particular salary and office space). They feel that by and large, neither the public nor the political leaders nor even their own superiors within the department are sympathetic to their position or helpful in times of stress.[52]

The police officer comes to learn that there are some people he can arrest and others he cannot. One officer in Rochester took great pride in ticketing the various officials' cars whenever they were double parked in front of city hall. The officer never reached a position higher than

---

[51] Daniel Dodsen, in *The Proceedings of the Institute of Police Community Relations* (East Lansing: Michigan State University, 1955), p. 75.

[52] Perry and Sornoff, *Politics at the Street Level*, p. 29, used by permission of the publisher.

motorcycle patrolman in his twenty-odd years on the force. The tickets were continually voided and the only reward the officer had was that of being recognized as gutsy by his peers.

Also, police officers in Rochester resented having to go out and "get some parking violators because the unit quota is not being met this month." Such a command may come at evening roll call, and it is understood that these parking violations will be obtained in the relatively "safe" white neighborhoods. The officers are not to give too many tickets in the black areas for fear of starting an incident. They resented the order to enforce laws at arbitrary rates and apply the enforcement of laws selectively.

Finally, the paramilitary structure of police bureaucracies also alienates the patrolman from administrators.

> The beat patrolman is relegated to corresponding with the rest of the agency through strict hierarchical chain of command. For example, the individual patrolman in the vast hierarchy of police departments must follow a strict chain of command when registering grievances about his job, even if such grievances concern his immediate superior. More precisely, as the President's Commission on Law Enforcement and Administration of Justice asks: "How does a patrolman go about telling his supervisor that he suspects the supervisor is being paid off by organized crime?" [53]

Perry and Sornoff add in this vein:

> For another example, while guest lecturing to a group of thirty New York City policemen (virtually all of whom were "front-line bureaucrats" or beat patrolmen), we learned that the recent Knapp Commission hearings on corruption in the New York Police Department were viewed by these men as little more than a "laff-a-minute" off-Broadway show rife with black humor. For when two of their number had recently—and properly—filed a corrupt practices complaint against an administrative superior, the latter official had them thrown in jail on the basis of his filing his own corrupt practices complaint against the beat patrolmen, thus, neutralizing the situation and setting in motion the well-known process of administrative "whitewash." [54]

In another context, patrolmen are, in a sense, products, if not victims, of their own racial and class characteristics and attitudes. Their attitudes concerning blacks and their identification with the aspirations to the life style and values of the middle class are important elements of their working

---

[53] Ibid., p. 15, used by permission.

[54] Ibid., used by permission.

personality. In fact, as table 6-9 demonstrates, the police officer, with few exceptions, could serve as a model representative of the OIC community. His income is higher than the OIC resident's because he is more prone to moonlight (or have another salary earner in the family), and he is more dissatisfied with his neighborhood because he is more dissatisfied with society in general. This dissatisfaction in large measure can be attributed to the police officers' experiences on the job. But outside of these characteristics, the basic social and economic characteristics of the police officers are very similar to those of the OIC residents.

TABLE 6-9

Social and Economic Characteristics of the Patrolmen and
the OIC and IC Representative Census Tracts

	Police	OIC	IC
Characteristic Ethnicity			
White (%)	100.0	100.0	24.8
Non-White (%)	——	——	75.2
Irish (%)	31.2	32.5	5.1
German (%)	25.0	26.3	4.4
Family Status			
Married Heads (%)	93.8	91.2	69.3
Single Heads (%)	6.2	8.7	30.6
Median Number Children	3.25	3.5	3.25
Age			
Median Age of Heads (Years)	——	48.0	28.5
Length Residence			
Median Length (Years)	20.58	20.47	10.0
Education			
Median No. Years School			
Completed	12.44	12.42	11.75
Housing			
Own (%)	62.5	68.4	21.2
Rent (%)	37.5	31.5	78.8
Income			
Median Family ($)	9,600	9,000	6,860
More than One Breadwinner (%)	75.0	39.4	35.0

Source: David C. Perry and Paula A. Sornoff, *Politics at the Street Level: The Select Case of Police Administration and the Community* (Beverly Hills, Calif.: Sage Publications, 1973).

Such similarities form a basic foundation for greater understanding of the citizens and complaints of the OIC than of the minority poor community. Further, in the Rochester study, it was discovered that the police officers had internalized OIC values and norms relative to the values and attitudes of the IC community. In a follow-up essay on this study it was argued that such a situation forces the (officer) in his role as an enforcer of the law, into the untenable position of being a captive of the values of the community in which he lives to the exclusion of seriously considering the values of the community in which he works (the IC community). . . . The lack of a substantial number of shared values between the unit patrolman and the IC clientele detracts from the potential for a common base of understanding when the patrolman is serving the minority/poor. This not to say that because the police do not exhibit or experience the same social and economic patterns of the IC residents, they will never provide accurate and responsive service. It merely points up the fact that the common base of similar life styles is present between the police and the OIC as the cornerstone upon which responsive service and clientele satisfaction could be facilitated.[55]

It is not clear whether the close approximation of socioeconomic white middle-class characteristics among the police has any direct effect upon the attitudes of police towards minority group citizens. However, there is evidence that police in general exhibit an overall prejudice toward nonwhite residents. In a nationwide study of fifteen cities in the United States,[56] the President's Commission observed the behavior of 604 police officers, both black and white. The data from this study is displayed in table 6-10. The officers are identified not only by race, but also by the racial composition of the precinct they work in. Their attitudes toward blacks are broken into six categories: "highly prejudiced, extremely anti-Negro;" "prejudiced, anti-Negro;" "neutral;" "pro-Negro;" "difficult to obtain information;" and "no relevant observation." The last two categories catalogue either the inability of the observer to obtain any observations of some police officers' attitudes toward blacks or the simple lack of the display of such attitudes by some officers.

The following describes the categories used:

[The "highly prejudiced, extremely anti-Negro" officer is exemplified by such statements as] "These scum aren't people; they're animals in a jungle." "Hitler had the right idea. We oughta gas these niggers—they're ruining the country." "Bastard savages." "Maggots." "Filthy pigs." "They oughta ship 'em back where they came from." "Buffaloes."

An officer was placed in the second category—"prejudiced or anti-Negro"—if he simply showed general dislike for Negroes as a group without making "extreme" statements as in the first category: "These people don't

---

[55] Ibid., p. 23, used by permission.

[56] The President's Commission on Law Enforcement and Administration of Justice, *Field Surveys III: Studies in Crime and Law Enforcement in Major Metropolitan Areas*, Vol. 2 (Washington, D.C.: Government Printing Office, 1967), pp. 132-39.

TABLE 6-10

Police Attitudes toward Blacks

Racial Composition of Police Precinct	Race of Officer	Total Number	Officer Attitude toward Negroes						Total Percent
			Highly Prejudiced, Extremely Anti-Black	Prejudiced, Anti-Black	Neutral	Pro-Black	Difficult to Obtain Information	No Relevant Observation	
Total	White	510	38	34	11	1	3	13	100
	Black	94	4	14	30	16	12	24	100
Predominantly Black	White	181	45	34	10	1	1	9	100
	Black	43	9	19	21	7	16	28	100
Racially Mixed	White	180	34	32	10	1	4	19	100
	Black	51	——	10	36	24	8	22	100
Predominantly White	White	149	36	36	13	2	3	11	100
	Black	——	——	——	——	——	——	——	——

SOURCE: The President's Commission on Law Enforcement and Administration of Justice, *Field Surveys III: Studies in Crime and Law Enforcement in Major Metropolitan Areas, Vol. 2* (Washington, D.C.: Government Printing Office, 1967), p. 135.

have enough respect for law and order." "Most of these niggers are too lazy to work for a living." "The trouble with shines is the way they run down a neighborhood—it's a real shame."

The third category—"neutral"—was used for an officer who spoke of Negroes descriptively, without judging them. He neither condemned nor defended Negroes, their advocates, or their critics: "The colored are about like anybody else." "The main problem is education—Negroes just don't get enough schooling." "There are all kinds of coloreds, some good, some bad."

The "pro-Negro" officer was outwardly sympathetic toward Negroes, or he defended Negroes against their critics: "These people deserve all the help they can get." "A.D.C. discriminates against Negroes." "They've been kept down too long. It's a disgrace for this country.[57]

From this information characteristics of police perceptions of the minority/poor clientele can be identified. First, more than two-thirds of the white police officers observed by the Commission staff, regardless of the specific clientele group they are servicing, expressed highly prejudiced or prejudiced attitudes toward blacks, while only 1-2 percent of white officers, regardless of the race of their patrol precinct, exhibited "pro-Negro" attitudes. Only among black police officers in the racially-mixed precincts were there more police officers who exhibited "pro-Negro" feelings than feelings of prejudice toward blacks. In fact, the highest level

[57] Ibid., pp. 133-34.

of anti-black feeling among black officers was found among those who service predominantly black precincts. Here, four times as many black officers exhibited prejudice toward fellow blacks than exhibited support of the ghetto residents.[58]

The Commission reports two basic conclusions from these data: (1) that the police servicing the residents of predominantly black neighborhoods exhibit more highly prejudiced attitudes, and (2) "policemen relate to Negroes as members of an organization, an organization with a belief system and goals of its own rather than as individuals." [59]

As pointed out in the discussion of clientele attitudes, attitudes such as these should not be construed as an indication of how police officers will necessarily behave in the minority/poor communities. In fact, there is often a directly inverse relation between what a police officer says about people when he is going to a call and how he behaves after he gets there. In the study of Rochester, for example, it was observed that the most highly prejudicial or racist language was used by police officers either when driving to a call which held a high potential for violence or when discussing a call in the station house after a violent or potentially violent situation. In fact, such dehumanizing words as "niggers," "buffaloes," and "jungle bunnies" were used when driving to a dangerous call in the black community and similar terms ("punks," "mics," "greasy little wops") were also used in the white community when a dangerous call emanated from that sector of the city. It may be that some of this language is not so much deliberately discriminatory as it is an attempt to put distance between the officer and the humanness of a client so that the use of violence to effect an arrest or bring order will be less painful or dislodging.

Such a discussion is not meant to explain away the overriding pattern of racial insensitivity which pervades American police departments. Rather, it is used to explain the unnervingly warlike situations which are sometimes part of the police officer's day in the street. The racial cleavages between minority citizens and the police are strong and painfully accurate indicators of racial tensions and disparities in the metropolis.

In short, the patrolman is a product of his environment and the goals and values he believes it should have. In a community with different racial characteristics, different lifestyles, and with a lack of observable evidence of the goals and values he finds important, the police officer is not only considered an alien interloper but also feels himself to be a foreigner as well. He may exhibit highly prejudicial or racist attitudes toward members of the ghetto community. Whether such attitudes are a product

---

[58] Ibid., pp. 132-39.

[59] Ibid., p. 138.

of the higher probability that he will meet such residents on calls of high risk, or a product of his own racially different environment, or a product of his incomplete training is not clear. What is clear is that there is a significant level of antagonism between many police officers and many residents of the minority/poor communities of the city.

The Police Function as a
Profession and a
Life Style

Very few professions in this country are carried out in relative isolation from other functionaries and have as part of their service potential control over the life or death of another person. In fact, other than the soldier, the most obvious examples are those of the doctor and the police officer. While both the doctor and the police officer carry on many of their functions with the help of well-defined teams of cohorts, many of their most sensitive functions are fragile relationships with patients and citizens carried on alone.

The Police as Professionals.   Given the broad range of functions of the police officer and the importance of such functions to the lives of citizens and the preservation of an orderly society, there has been much attention placed upon the professional nature of the police function. Like a doctor, the police officer has that attribute of a professional which is characterized by the exercise of "wide discretion alone and with respect to matters of the greatest importance." [60]

However, as discussed earlier, many attempts are made to remove the police officer from a discretionary role in the administration of law and order on the streets. For all practical purposes, the police officer is to rely on his code: his "clean ruggedness" and his duty to provide "emotion-free" service to all persons in the same manner. Such theory is highly impractical in its recognition of what really occurs on the street. Yet it is adhered to rather rigorously by most police departments because the "professional" preparation of the police officer is so shallow that, for the most part, the administrator dares not allow the average patrolman discretion to approach the street without tens of thousands of laws and administrative rulings to guide his every action and a constant paramilitary admonition that the police officers maintain an emotionless uniformed sameness during encounters with citizens on the street.

Jesse Rubin points out that

---

[60] Wilson, *Varieties of Police Behavior*, p. 24.

there is general agreement that a professional is someone who achieves the privilege of exercising discretion within his field of competence only through discipline, training, and apprenticeship. He must subject himself to the discipline of the profession as well as to the discipline inherent in his organizational structure. In terms of its requirements, policing is a profession, but police training generally falls very far short of coming within such a definition.[61]

Where lip service is paid to such discipline through the paramilitary organization of the police and through codes of "clean ruggedness," the emphasis in training is placed on handling a gun, becoming physically fit, and learning many laws and various record-keeping techniques. Beyond this, training programs are as different as the styles and types of police departments in the metropolis. The International Association of Police Chiefs pointed out that, as of 1965, "less than 15 percent of all agencies surveyed, . . . provided immediate training for recruits, about half provided it 'as soon as possible' within the first year." [62]

Of these departments who do provide at least recruit training, the training is far from adequate. Where tasks such as those of a doctor, priest, or rabbi take years of specialized and grueling education and training, the average police officer can expect about eight weeks of training. In such a short period it is highly doubtful whether such programs

provide recruits with an ample understanding of the police task. For example, very few of the training programs . . . provide course material on the history of law enforcement, the role of police in modern society, or the need for discretion in law enforcement. . . . Current training programs, for the most part, prepare an officer to perform police work mechanically, but do not prepare him to understand his community, the police role, or the imperfections of the criminal justice system.[63]

Almost without exception the instructors in police academies are products of the same faulty system—they are other officers trained and brought through the ranks of the police department. They are expected to perform in a few hours the miracle of turning young men into sophisticated agents of social control who can balance the highly touted goals of their job as discussed in the clean and orderly environment of the classroom with the raw and emotional world of the street. Such a task is an awesome

---

[61] Jesse Rubin, "Police Identity and Police Role," in *The Police and the Community*, ed. Robert F. Steadman (Baltimore: The Johns Hopkins University Press, 1972), p. 22.

[62] Ibid.

[63] Ibid.

job, and when it is taught by officers who are a product of the past failures of such a system, the training of police can become a process of reinforced inadequacies. The recruit is alternately barraged with the boring task of learning precise record-keeping techniques and legal statutes and with the highly generalized polemics of "how important his job is." Such differing approaches to the police role leave the police recruit in a quandry—on the one hand his job is portrayed as a boring and seemingly endless task of writing out forms and learning laws and on the other hand he is told that he is some sort of a "savior in blue."

Arthur Niederhoffer points out that once the police recruit hits the street, even good training becomes difficult to apply:

> The new patrolman must resolve the dilemma of choosing between the professional ideal of police work he has learned at the academy and the pragmatic precinct approach. In the academy, where professionalism is accented, the orientation is toward that of the social sciences as opposed to the lock-them-up philosophy, but in the precinct the patrolman is measured by his arrest record. Thus, the new man is needed when he shows signs of diffidence in arresting or asserting his authority. Over and over again, well-meaning old timers reiterate, "Ya gotta be tough kid, or you'll never last." [64]

It is not reassuring to consider that police officers, with the ability to change a person's life through an arrest and through the type of record such an action can set in motion, are so poorly trained. Coupled with this poor training are their prejudices and their conflict-ridden role vis-à-vis the rest of society. Together these characteristics of police on the street demonstrate what a short distance American government has come in providing its citizens with even the most fundamental service of law enforcement. To place the blame at the feet of the police officers solely is an act of abdication of responsibility for the institutionalized inconsistencies and outright inequities which permeate public police administration in America.

The Police Officer Alone.   In the preceding sections it was argued that the police officer is a product, and perhaps a victim, of societal complexity and disparities, the inconsistencies inherent in the job of police officer, his own life style, values ·and attitudes, and his "professional" training. As these cross-cutting pressures mount, the officer retreats into a state

---

[64] Arthur Niederhoffer, *Behind the Shield* (Garden City, N.Y.: Doubleday, 1967), pp. 52-53.

of "social isolation." [65] Jonathan Rubinstein succinctly sums up the day-to-day experience of being a cop in the following manner:

> The policeman is a solitary worker. The nature of his trade requires that he spend a good part of his work day alone; the nature of his obligation isolates him from most other people. . . . He has little opportunity to maintain friendships with people who are not policemen. . . . Inevitably, his close friends, if he has any, are some of the men from his platoon and squad. [66]

In a very real sense the police officer does the unpleasant work of society. If a police officer is afraid of heights, getting a cat out of a tree is a difficult task and his fear will incur the rath of the anxious cat-owner. If a police officer does not respond quickly enough to the demands of a situation where a person has suffered a coronary, the relatives of the deceased will not sing his praises as a doctor or even as a paramedic. These types of situations, coupled with the serious problems of disorder, crime and race and class indiscretions on the part of police, all lead to an attitude among police that the public in general has a negative view of them personally and also of the type of job they do. [67]

Beyond the tasks which the public directly knows that the policeman performs are tasks which are only alluded to and which also add to the rather onerous image the police officer feels the public paints of him. These include letting certain illegal actions continue to occur because, for example, only through letting small drug traffickers continue to deal can they get to the "big ones," or because "city hall" wants certain violations in certain areas to go untouched. Also, they know of colleagues who are on the take, or they may be themselves. [68] They must perform tasks which may entail the taking of a life. They see life at its worst and are often so repulsed that they strike back. Such actions may later haunt the officer as much as the persons he finds repulsive. None of these experiences are easily shared with or sympathetically received by outsiders—whether such outsiders be members of the relatively sympathetic

---

[65] Skolnick, *Justice Without Trial*, pp. 49-51.

[66] Jonathan Rubinstein, *City Police* (New York: Farrar, Straus, and Giroux, 1973), p. 434.

[67] Perry, "Police Service in a Dual Society," chapter 5: Bayley and Mendelsohn, *Minorities and the Police*, chapter 2, and Rubin, "Police Identity and Police Role" in *The Police and the Community*, ed. Steadman.

[68] Rubinstein, *City Police*, pp. 435-36; also see Dodsen, in *The Proceedings of the Institute of Police Community Relations*.

white community or his own family. Hence the officer retreats within himself.

One sergeant in Rochester discussed this experience of social isolation during his leisure hours. He said that he had not been to a party or social gathering outside of a family party or gathering of police families in eight years. When asked to explain this pattern of socializing, he said:

> Look, if you ever want to "queer" a party, just walk in and when the first person asks you what you do for a living—tell him you're a cop. The conversation will stop. The ice will not tinkle in the glass any more and people will go to the other side of the room. Everyone in that room had a mother who threatened that they'd get turned over to the cops if they didn't eat their spinach—you know what I mean? And half of them will go out of that party and not be able to pass a breathalizer test. You've been spoilin' their fun right now by "spyn" on them at their party. You're a spy by just bein' there.[69]

The patrolman just "knows" that people really only want him around when they are in trouble. The rest of the time the police officer is basically not appreciated—not even by the white communities of the metropolis who allegedly support them. And in the black community, given the composite of institutionalized inequities which the police officer represents as an agent of government, just his presence is antagonizing, no matter how responsive he personally tries to be.

As a result of this isolation from the world around him, the police officer turns to his fellow officers for support both on the job and during his leisure hours. In the company of his colleagues he finds the support which citizens on the street will not give even when he is himself in trouble.[70] As one patrolman interviewed by Skolnick said:

> Jerry, a cop, can get into a fight with three or four tough kids, and there will be citizens passing by, and maybe they'll look, but they'll never lend a hand. It's their country too, but you'd never know it the way some of them act. They forget that we're made of flesh and blood too. They don't care what happens to the cop so long as they don't get a little dirty.[71]

The police officer does not want to fight society's battle for law and order alone. He feels that just as the first constables could deputize citizens to come to their aid, he too should at least be able to count upon the

---

[69] Perry, "Police in a Dual Society," interview notes.

[70] Ibid., p. 53.

[71] Skolnick, *Justice Without Trial*, p. 50.

citizens around him for help in a tight spot. Yet the dilemma is a common one for the police officer and hence he learns to depend and trust only those who understand—and those who understand best are his colleagues.

This bond of solidarity on the job becomes a strong tie to off-the-job relationships. In the fourteen months of field work with the Rochester police force, the author never attended a social event hosted by a police officer in which there were more than a handful of non-officers. Most of these non-officers were members of the primary or extended family of one officer or another.

It is argued that such solidarity among police has become an important part of the police officer's personality.[72] Yet on the job, while the patrolman may be more open with his fellow police officers than with others, he does not even trust most of his fellow officers. This is the case for a variety of reasons. First, the bulk of the patrolman's job is carried on *alone* or with only one other officer (his partner in a car). If he is to make an arrest or gain information which will be used in arrest (and hence gain him favor with his superiors) he must gather this information and keep it to himself. He will not give the information to someone who he cannot be sure will either be helpful in his project or who will not willingly share with him any awards that may accrue from his activities. Hence, with heavy inter-precinct and intra-departmental competition for the few rewards which can be gained in the police force, the policeman must protect what resources he has and put them to good advantage only with those he *knows* he can trust. Second, if the police officer is engaged in some illegal practice or even if he is not, he must act to protect himself concerning such practices. He must be sure that the secrecy and privacy of the illegal acts is not disturbed.[73] Through experiences like this, the most intimate relationship the police officer develops is with his car or wagon partner. They spend many hours alone together, and they must learn to trust each other.

Summary

The metropolises of today are torn by a series of diversely characterized communities evidencing varying levels of satisfaction over the way in which the police are operating. The police of many central city and outside central city forces are ill-trained to take on highly discretionary functions of the role which serves the most fundamental need of the individual and the society. The individual officer often finds little support for the

---

[72] William A. Westley, "Secrecy and the Police," *Social Forces* 34 (1956): 254-57.

[73] Rubinstein, *City Police*, p. 438.

rigors of his job in either the black or white communities of the city, even though there is at least tacit support from the white community. He is an ambassador entering a foreign land when he enters many sectors of the black ghetto—he does not understand the people and he is a representative of a government which allegedly refuses to meet with any sense of vigor the demands of the people.

He believes that he is fast becoming an outcast in his own city and even with his own people. At the time when the challenges of his job seem to be greater than ever before, the levels of support and the prestige which the police officer can take from his job are exceedingly low. The police officer feels used by just about everyone he meets on the street. The middle class will support the police officer but does not accept him socially. To many minority group members, the present police officer will never be accepted as anything more than a marginal public servant who represents very little in the way of real protection for the minority/poor community. The police officer is often more of a threat to the community than a protector. Even his own colleagues are not to be trusted with the policeman's professional and personal problems, and not even his family would respond favorably to much that he knows or does. Hence, he carries many of his burdens alone.

For all this, his pay in many communities is so low that the police officer must moonlight on a second job in order to make ends meet. In fact, the head of the police benevolent association in Rochester said one day that if police officers were told they could not moonlight in Rochester, then "you would see 400 of our 600 police officers on the unemployment lines the next day—they couldn't continue to be cops without the second job to support them."

In short, the police officer carries a staggering burden with little training, pay, support, and self-esteem. While he may be personally guilty of unresponsive service or brutality, it is more likely that his lack of response or short temper are products of conditions over which he has limited control, and he remains, in part, a victim of these conditions.

Conclusion

Most contemporary treatments of the police spend at least a few pages and sometimes much more offering reforms or changes in the public policy process. The subject matter here, however, is too broad to engage in such a task. To offer suggestions for change here would be to undertake an argument for social reform which would cut across the entire sweep of the American metropolis.

The well-worked platitude, a chain is as strong as its weakest link, applies well here. Changes are needed at the street level to better prepare and guide the individual police officer and for the government and financing of the law enforcement function. The police function is in need of change from the street to the city hall to the county seat to the state house to Washington, D.C. As such, its present-day successes and shortcomings are revealing indicators of the interrelated strengths and weaknesses of metropolitan America.

Index